WORLD BANK STAFF OCCASIONAL PAPERS NUMBER TWENTY

Alvin C. Egbert
Hyung M. Kim

A Development Model
for the
Agricultural Sector
of Portugal

Published for the World Bank
THE JOHNS HOPKINS UNIVERSITY PRESS
BALTIMORE AND LONDON

Library of Congress Cataloging in Publication Data:

Egbert, Alvin Charles, 1922–
    A development model for the agricultural sector of Portugal.

    (World Bank staff occasional papers; no. 20)
    Bibliography: p. 95.
    1. Agriculture—Economic aspects—Portugal—Mathematical models.
2. Agriculture and state—Portugal—Mathematical models.
I. Kim, Hyung M., 1937–   joint author. II. Title. III. Series.
HD2027.E35   338.1'09469   75-26662
ISBN 0-8018-1793-5

Foreword

I would like to explain why the World Bank does research work and why this research is published. We feel an obligation to look beyond the projects that we help finance toward the whole resource allocation of an economy and the effectiveness of the use of those resources. Our major concern, in dealings with member countries, is that all scarce resources—including capital, skilled labor, enterprise, and know-how—should be used to their best advantage. We want to see policies that encourage appropriate increases in the supply of savings, whether domestic or international. Finally, we are required by our Articles, as well as by inclination, to use objective economic criteria in all our judgments.

These are our preoccupations, and these, one way or another, are the subjects of most of our research work. Clearly, they are also the proper concern of anyone who is interested in promoting development, and so we seek to make our research papers widely available. In doing so, we have to take the risk of being misunderstood. Although these studies are published by the Bank, the views expressed and the methods explored should not necessarily be considered to represent the Bank's views or policies. Rather, they are offered as a modest contribution to the great discussion on how to advance the economic development of the underdeveloped world.

ROBERT S. McNAMARA
President
The World Bank

Preface

The World Bank is now the largest external provider of funds to promote agricultural development in the developing countries of the world. The Bank also conducts a continuous dialogue with the governments of these countries about the most appropriate strategies for improvement in the agricultural sector. Consequently, Bank staff work continuously to evolve more appropriate tools for, and methods of, economic analysis to help pinpoint such optimal strategies.

Although these analytical tools and methods are constantly being improved, in the Bank and elsewhere, the need for sound, precise analysis still exceeds our capacity. The study undertaken by Alvin C. Egbert and Hyung M. Kim and reported here represents an attempt to develop comprehensive and quantitative methods to support strategies in agricultural sector development. The study uses mathematical programming to specify development strategies and investment requirements, through 1980, for homogeneous agricultural production regions in Portugal. Among the unique features are the specification of product demand functions for each region at the retail level and the joint analysis of agricultural processing industries and on-farm production.

The opening chapter of the study, which otherwise is presented on a technical level, was written with the lay reader in mind. It contains an overview of the study in nontechnical language, covering the general character of the analysis and of the agricultural situation and summarizing the principal findings and conclusions of the project.

The study was carried out in collaboration with the Center for Agricultural Economic Studies of the Calouste Gulbenkian Foundation of Lisbon. Mario Pereira, director of the Center, made this collaboration possible and provided encouragement and counsel throughout the study. Fernando Estácio and Cortez Lobão worked as direct collaborators since the project agreement was signed in March 1971. Their detailed knowledge of the resource base, present cultural practices, and marketing structure of Portuguese agriculture was especially valuable. Moreover, they obtained essential information, much of it unpublished, from many government agencies and supervised the assembly of inputs and outputs for production activities. Many others at the Center also provided counsel and guidance, as well as basic data used to assemble input-output coefficients.

The authors are grateful to Jean Waelbroeck of the World Bank and to an anonymous reviewer, both of whom improved this report with their comments. Acknowledgment is also due to Hilda Villanasco, Emma Trenchi, and Elizabeth Mico, who typed the several drafts. The manuscript was edited by Goddard W. Winterbottom; Rachel C. Anderson coordinated the book production.

MONTAGUE YUDELMAN
Director
Agriculture and Rural
Development Department

Washington, D.C.
July 1975

Contents

A Development Model
for the
Agricultural Sector
of Portugal

1

Introduction and Summary

The World Bank and other development institutions are faced with the difficult task of estimating the actual impact of project loans on the economic growth of developing countries. In recent years there has been increasing recognition that conventional methods of appraising projects do not invariably lead to the financing of the best development projects. As a result, general studies of education, agriculture, transportation, and other economic or social sectors have been undertaken to identify programs and projects that might be more effective in promoting growth in these sectors.

The usual procedure for these sector studies has been to send a survey team of from five to ten persons to a country for from six to eight weeks. During this time the team tours the countryside, talks to government officials and agricultural specialists, and collects data. It then spends several months in the Bank analyzing data and writing a report. In that period of time such a team of specialists can obtain a general picture of the sector and make qualitative recommendations, but it is not likely that they can make quantitative recommendations. Even if they are able to do so, the separate and uncoordinated recommendations may not be achievable because resources to carry them out may not be available in the country.

This study represents an attempt to make recommendations on sector development that are quantitative and at the same time consistent with the resource endowment of a country. It was conceived and initiated when the Bank sent a team to Portugal in 1969 to carry out a conventional sector survey.

The general objective of the analysis reported here was to determine

3

whether a certain type of model could produce better insight into the mechanics of agricultural development, one that would lead to the design of improved agricultural development strategies and programs. The study comprised four phases. First, a spatial equilibrium programming model was developed and tested, using 1968 data and other relevant information. Briefly, a spatial equilibrium programming model assumes that an economy can be divided into separate geographical regions of economic activity and that economic forces are at work so that prices between each separate market differ by no more than transport cost. Eleven such regional markets, covering all of Portugal, were defined for the study. Second, two simplified models, one partial and the other aggregative, were designed and tested to determine the types and magnitudes of errors that could result from using such simplified models. Third, the eleven-region model was used to specify investment programs for Portugal's agriculture through 1980. Fourth, these investment programs were compared with the recommendations that had been made in the survey mission's report to the Portuguese government.

Similar studies have been carried out by Bank personnel in collaboration with other countries. One, which was part of this project, was done for Brazil.[1] But because of an inadequate data base, the results did not turn out well. A more economywide study of Mexico was done by the Development Research Center (DRC) of the Bank and published in 1973.[2] Work is continuing on this project to improve its structure and results. The DRC also has done a dynamic, broad regional and sectoral study of the Ivory Coast that emphasizes agriculture and education.[3]

It is not possible at this time to determine the relative merits of these alternative sector studies. Those which include more sectors are usually preferred. But each study has its own unique objective and a gain in one objective usually requires the sacrifice of another. From a research point of view, the best procedure for comparison would be to apply each analysis to the same country and compare results, including costs.

1. Gottfried Ablasser and Alvin C. Egbert, "Brazil Agricultural Sector Planning Model: An Application of Mathematical Regional Programming," Agriculture and Rural Development Department Working Paper no. 1 (Washington: World Bank, December 1973).

2. Louis M. Goreux and Alan S. Manne (eds.), *Multi-Level Planning: Case Studies in Mexico* (Amsterdam: North Holland, 1973).

3. Louis M. Goreux, *Multi-Level Programming in the Ivory Coast* (in preparation).

Because of the cost involved in such an undertaking, however, this is not likely to be done.

THE AGRICULTURAL SECTOR OF PORTUGAL

The agricultural sector in Portugal has performed comparatively poorly in recent years. The annual growth between 1960 and 1974 averaged about 0.9 percent, or slightly greater than the annual growth of population, 0.8 percent. At first glance this rate might appear quite satisfactory, but the demand for food grew faster than population, at 1.8 percent, because of rising per capita incomes. It is the contrast of this 1.8 percent growth in the demand for food to the 0.9 percent growth in production that is of concern to the government.

The widening gap between agricultural output and domestic demand has resulted in a rapid rise of imports of food and feed products—of beef, wheat, and corn in particular. On the other hand, possibilities are not great for expanding such traditional exports as olive oil and wine. There was a large expansion of exports of tomato products—a non-traditional export—in the late 1960s, but the U.S. market for these products declined and recent export growth has been slow.

A major inhibitor of the growth of Portuguese agriculture is the quality of the resource base. The fertility of the soil is low. The hilly or mountainous topography in the northern half and in the southern strip of the country known as the Algarve makes much of the land unsuitable or impracticable for cropping. In the potentially more productive Alentejo region of the south, in which the topography is gently rolling and favorable for cultivation, rainfall averages only between 500 and 800 millimeters (12.5 and 20 inches) a year, most of it during the winter season, and much of the area is semiarid. Output per hectare is higher in the north than in the south, in which cultivation is extensive, and much of the land is left idle for periods of from four to seven years to grow in native grasses, partly because of the poor distribution of rainfall and partly because of the belief of the farmers that the soil must be rested to restore fertility.

Most of the farmholdings in Portugal are small. More than 80 percent of the farms in the northern mountainous part of the country comprise less than three hectares; many of these are fragmented. Farms are similarly small in the central sections of the country near the Tejo River.

In the Alentejo, 50 percent of the farms comprise less than three hectares. But the large farms in this area—those of more than 50 hectares—account for only 6 percent of the number of farms yet cultivate more than 90 percent of the total agricultural area.

Production per hectare (yield) and per man-hour is relatively low throughout Portugal. Yields are higher in the north because of a higher labor input per hectare and higher rainfall. Low productivity throughout the country results not only from the poor land and climatic base but also from continual use of traditional methods of cultivation that employ large inputs of labor and low inputs of machinery, improved seeds, fertilizers, and pesticides. Much advanced technology, however, is available to stimulate agricultural growth, and research has shown that in many cases the output per hectare can be doubled or tripled by the use of commercial fertilizers and improved seeds.

As in other sectors of the economy, the government intervenes directly in much of the agricultural decisionmaking. The economy is mixed, having both free market and managed elements, but the latter seem to predominate. Agricultural markets are managed extensively through *juntas* (councils), commissions, and institutes. Farmers are organized under European-type guilds (*gremios de lavoura*), which are strongly influenced by governmental exhortation, subsidy, and price supports.

The government has established many incentive programs to encourage modern practices in inputs and production, including high price supports, seed and fertilizer subsidies, bonuses for feeding cattle to heavier weights before slaughter, and protection from foreign supplies. None of these, however, has yet had much impact on agricultural productivity.

Although Portugal appears to have considerable potential for improving the performance of its agricultural sector, the government must carefully evaluate its alternatives for agricultural development. First, it must know what particular areas of the country and what particular products have potential for improved economic performance. Second, it must find the most practical way or ways in which to persuade farmers to adopt the most favorable opportunities. Policies and institutions that at present inhibit growth—price policies and supply management, for example—must be changed.

The purpose of this study, however, was only to estimate where the greatest potentials for economic development lie and to quantify them as accurately as possible. Methods of implementing those specific programs and institutional change that may be required are outside its objectives.

ECONOMIC MODELING AND DEVELOPMENT PLANNING

The choice of the particular analytical method to be used for sector analysis depends on a number of factors. Among these are availability of data, nature of the economic and political system, and objectives of, and systems for, planning. A shortage or lack of relevant data, for example, will preclude the use of complex models. An economic system that allows for strong governmental intervention implies use of a model different from that for analyzing a free market economy. In a market economy the model must reflect producer and consumer behavior in response both to prices and to any governmental programs. In certain economies these variables (that is, programs) may include only monetary and fiscal instruments. Behavioral models must be estimated by statistical methods that require either historical or experimental data, and the latter cannot be obtained for economic situations. Thus, in those economic situations which warrant use of behavioral models but for which historical data are lacking, simulation techniques may be most appropriate. It is possible to use partial and synthesized data in simulation models and through the process of simulation and testing to determine their appropriateness for analysis.

An efficiency model such as mathematical programming seems more appropriate for the economy of Portugal, which is the object of much planning and governmental intervention. An efficiency model—given available resources, production technology, consumer income, and the nature of final product demand—specifies an efficient production, distribution, and consumption program for the economy or sector. The term "efficiency" as used here means that the price that consumers pay for each product in each market will be equal to the cost of supplying it to that market: of production, processing, transportation, and handling. The model does not assume that the unseen hand of the market will bring this optimal program into being; governmental direction and assistance will be necessary. This model implicitly assumes that the planning agency is interested in economic efficiency and income growth for all sectors of the economy, not for the agricultural sector alone. It assumes also that the planner requires detailed regional and commodity information in order to select appropriate projects. Thus, each type of economic datum is specified for each region.

The need for this type of information will depend on the options open to planners. The model is flexible, however, and can be used to evaluate trade controls, tariffs, programs for income reallocation, and similar factors. The specific model used for this analysis included all the basic agricultural resources—land, labor, machinery, standing trees, and so on—and twenty-six of the most important products of the agricultural sector. Only poultry, fruits, and vegetables were omitted.

SUMMARY OF RESULTS AND CONCLUSIONS

The results of the validation phase of the model, which used 1968 base data, were sufficiently encouraging to warrant completing the other three phases of the work more or less as planned.

Two types of simplified models were analyzed. The first was a partial, or two-region, model, one that made use of only two of the basic eleven regions. The second was a complete model for the entire country, in which the basic eleven regions and the data associated with each were aggregated to form just three regions.

The objective of the two-region model was to determine whether one area of a country could be planned by linear programming without serious differences in the results compared with those of the eleven-region model. Because the model is partial, the analyst must specify values for certain data—for example, prices of interregional imports—that are given to the solution to a countrywide model. For the results of a partial regional model and countrywide regional model to be the same (or reasonably so), these prescribed, or exogenous, data must be roughly equivalent to those generated by the countrywide model. For the analysis with the two-region model, the exogenous data were estimated based on 1968 values and historical trends. In comparisons of production, consumption, and prices the results show that in some cases the total model estimates the base period data with greater precision, whereas in other cases the partial model does better. But on balance the total model gave greater precision.

The aggregated three-region model was constructed to determine the types and amount of error that could result from customary methods of aggregating data over regions. The results show that these simple aggregation procedures can result in significant errors—and serious mistakes could thereby be introduced through the use of greatly aggregated programming models for all development planning. Significant errors can arise, first, because aggregation can prevent the programming specification of a crop, for example, for a small area of a region in which its productivity is highest; and, second, because those production activities which require unique water, soil, climate, and other resource characteristics may be specified by the model at unobtainable levels. By intraregional specification of resources by productivity class and by tying production activities to these resources, class by class, it appears possible to eliminate these errors to some degree and at the same time to maintain large regions for analysis.

The foregoing methodological results shed some light on the best procedure for sector planning. The most important result of the project is the analysis for 1980, the third phase, which evaluated the economic potential of possible investments and new production practices. Investment alternatives included irrigation, livestock herds together with requisite buildings and equipment, pine and eucalyptus forests, and tractors and other farm machinery. Two new crop alternatives, sunflower and safflower, were considered mainly as possible sources of high-protein feed, most of which has had to be imported.

Three steps to this analysis demonstrated the interdependency of agricultural investment decisions. In the first, called variant 1, capacities of the meat cold-storage processing were held at their 1968 level. Variant 2 permitted the cold-storage capacity to expand without limit, whereas variant 3 permitted both cold-storage capacity and plants for processing livestock products to expand without limit.

All of the investment alternatives except development of irrigation appear to have good economic potential in at least one of the eleven regions considered. For example, in one region four types of investment—farm machinery, dairy, beef, and sheep—were prescribed. In another region, only one—sheep herd development—was prescribed. The total level of investments over the planning period 1968–80 for the three alternatives increased successively from variant to variant, from 1.0 billion to 1.4 billion escudos ($40 million to $56 million), or a maximum of about $4 million per year.

The further development of irrigation does not appear profitable at the present time because of its high cost and because there seems to be a large potential for increasing the agricultural output from existing irrigated land and from rainfed agriculture through available improved production practices. These practices mainly include higher-yield seeds and larger rates of fertilization. If this unexploited potential were utilized, the country could meet virtually all of its own food needs and increase its agricultural balance-of-trade surplus, and at the same time divert marginal lands to forestry, recreation, and other uses. Total cropland programmed in the model for use in 1980 was 48 percent less than actual use in 1968. Moreover, under the three alternative solutions, there would be an improvement in the average diet, with more protein and less starchy food.

In the fourth phase the comparison of the programming results with the investment recommendations of the sector survey mission showed some qualitative similarities: both the program and the mission report contained recommendations in regard to eucalyptus forests, beef and sheep production, and cold-storage plants for meats—but only the eucalyptus recommendation was stated quantitatively by the mission. The mission did not recommend the development of swine production, processing for livestock products, pine forests, and facilities for processing forest products, all investments prescribed by the programming analysis. The mission did, however, recommend the development of port facilities, an area of investment not considered in the programming analysis. Finally, none of the mission's recommendations were earmarked for a particular region of the country, a requirement for good development planning.

The programming model used for this analysis was not developed to its fullest potential because of limitations of time and resources. Some regional demand functions needed to be adjusted to reflect market equilibrium for all commodities. No sales were specified for certain commodities in a few regions: the amount supplied could be sold for a price higher than the programmed price, or a greater amount could have been sold at a lower price. These defects could be corrected by minor adjustments in demand specifications. More fundamental defects included a lack of information on the variation in labor supply with labor price, a lack of a full range of investment activities for all replaceable fixed resources, and the static nature of the model. Given more time and resources, each of these defects are to a large degree correctable. But it was found through working with this model and a similar one for Brazil that, given present computers and software, computer cost rose sharply when the matrix size reached a certain limit: increasing the matrix size from 1,000 x 4,500 to 1,400 x 5,500 resulted, for example, in a sixfold increase in real computer time.

Because of the considerable amount of time required to assemble data for models of this type and the substantial cost involved, we do not recommend that the Bank carry out sector analyses of this type as a general practice. It could, however, offer technical assistance and some financial support to countries wishing to engage in such analyses, especially those countries in which sector studies are planned in the future. To a large degree, a programming study could replace a regular sector study. Moreover, once a model is implemented it can be revised and improved at a fraction of the original cost. Thus, country planning groups would do well to improve and continue to use such a model in developing sequential plans, a program that our collaborators in Portugal hope to implement.

Finally, the output of such models should not be considered infallible. The results are only as good as their structure and as the data that go into them. They do provide, however, a tremendous amount of detailed information that can and should be used in conjunction with other less complex studies.

2

The Spatial Equilibrium Programming Model

The model used for analysis follows, in general, the concepts laid out by Paul Samuelson.[1] But for practical reasons it involves a few minor differences (as will be seen shortly). In structure and data the model includes for each location (or region)[2] demand functions for all final products; processing activities that transform agricultural products into consumer goods; production activities that convert basic resources into agricultural products; transport activities that transfer raw materials and final products from each region to every other region; and import and export activities for selected products.

For programming, the objective of the model is to determine the regional production and consumption mix of products originating in the agriculture (domestic or foreign) that will maximize total producer and consumer surplus, given the level of consumer's income; the cost (both direct and opportunity) of production; cost of transportation between markets; and net export and import prices.

The solution to the model is such that the selling price of each final product in each region is equal to its total marginal cost for production, processing, handling, transport, and selling. The objective function of the programming model is characterized by Figure 1, which shows typical supply and demand, or market equilibrium, for a single product. The

---

1. Paul A. Samuelson, "Spatial Price Equilibrium and Linear Programming," *American Economic Review*, vol. 42 (1952), pp. 283–303.

2. In spatial equilibrium models unique functions, variables, and parameters are specified for each location or region.

Figure 1. Consumer's and Producer's Surplus in Market Equilibrium

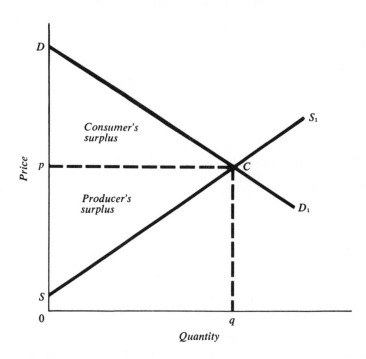

triangle *PCD* represents consumers' surplus, which is the difference between the marginal value of each succeeding unit, as expressed by the demand curve DD_1 and what the consumers must pay, price *P*, for a commodity. Similarly, the producers' surplus, represented by triangle *PCS*, is the difference between the price received for the product and the marginal production cost of each succeeding unit, which is expressed by supply curve SS_1. It is possible, of course, that marginal cost and average unit costs are constant, as a result of which the producers' surplus is zero. Supply curves in the model to be presented are step functions and can only be graphed a posteriori because the nature of the supply curve is determined only in the final equilibrium solution.

This means that the supply curve SS_1 in Figure 1, which is determined by marginal unit cost, may take different shapes and levels from solution to solution. The demand curves, however, remain the same because they are determined only by the level of income and population that is constant or exogenous in the model. The supply curves, on the other hand, are functions not only of production, transport, and processing costs, which are constants, but also of the prices of other competing products that are endogenous and variable in the analysis. (An example of market equilibrium generated by a model solution is given in Figure 3.)

MATHEMATICAL STRUCTURE

In mathematical language the model is defined by equations (1) through (8), in which all exogenous or predetermined variables and matrix coefficients are labeled with an asterisk.

The objective function of the model is:

(1) $\text{Max } f(w) = \sum_i \sum_j S_{ij} \lambda_{ij}$

$$+ \sum_i \sum_j (EP)_{ij}{}^* (EX)_{ij} - \sum_m \sum_j (PC)_{mj}{}^* M_{mj}$$

$$- \sum_p \sum_j C_{pj}{}^* P_{pj} - \sum_i \sum_j (IP)_{ij}{}^* (IM)_{ij}$$

$$- \sum_m \sum_j \sum_{\substack{j' \\ j \neq j'}} T_{mjj'} t_{mjj'}{}^* - \sum_i \sum_j \sum_{\substack{j' \\ j \neq j'}} T_{rjj'} t_{rjj'}{}^*$$

$$- \sum_i \sum_j \sum_{\substack{j' \\ j \neq j'}} T_{ijj'} t_{ijj'}{}^*,$$

where $f(w)$ is a scalar representing net social payoff; S_{ij} is the amount of product i sold in jth region; i equals $1 \ldots X$; j equals $1 \ldots Y$; λ_{ij} is average utility measured in dollars derived from the ith product in the jth region, which is a function of the level of income, I_j, and the amount consumed, S_{ij}; $(EP)_{ij}$ is the net price of product i exported [3] from the jth region; $(EX)_{ij}$ is the amount of product i exported from jth region; $(PC)_{mj}$ is the unit cost of converting primary agricultural products, m, into consumer or final products; m equals $1, \ldots, Z$; M_{mj} is the amount of primary product, m, processed in jth region; P_{pj} is the level of primary production activity, p, in jth region (each primary production activity may produce more than one primary product, m); p equals $1, \ldots, \alpha$; C_{pj} is the unit cost of the pth primary production activity in the jth region; $(IP)_{ij}$ is the total import price of product i in the jth region; $(IM)_{ij}$ is the level of import of product i in the jth region; $T_{mjj'}$ is the

---

3. The terms "imports" and "exports" refer to trade with other countries; the term "shipment" refers to interregional trade.

amount of primary product, m, transported from region j to region j' (since intraregional transport is not considered $j \neq j'$); and $t_{mjj'}$ is the cost of transporting one unit of primary product m from region j to region j' ($i' = 1, 2, \ldots, J$).

In the other similar transport terms in equation (1) the subscript r refers to basic resources ($r = 1, \ldots, B$), and as noted above i refers to final products or consumer goods.

In summary, equation (1) states that the objective of the programming model is to maximize the total net social payoff—producer and consumer welfare—of domestic sales plus the value of exports of goods originating in agriculture, given the level of consumer income in each region.

The maximization of equation (1) is constrained by available resources, market balance, and other conditions, as follows:

$$(2) \quad R^*_{jr} \geq \sum_p a^*_{pjr} P_{pj} + \sum_m a^*_{mjr} M_{mj} + \sum_{\substack{j' \\ j \neq j}} T_{rjj'} - \sum_{\substack{j \\ j \neq j'}} T_{rjj'}.$$

Equation (2) states that the amount of basic resource, r, used by the primary production and processing activities, plus the amount shipped into region j, minus the amount shipped out, cannot exceed the fixed supply, R_{jr}.

$$(3) \quad 0 \geq \sum_p \pm b^*_{pjm} P_{pj} + M_{mj} + \sum_{\substack{j' \\ j' \neq j}} T_{mjj'} - \sum_{\substack{j \\ j \neq j'}} T_{rjj'}.^4$$

Equation (3) states that the amount of primary product m processed in region j cannot exceed the net amount produced in the region by production activities P_{pj}, plus the amount shipped in, minus the amount shipped out.

$$(4) \quad 0 \geq -b^*_{ijm} M_j + S_{ij} + (EX)_{ij} - (IM)_{ij} + \sum_{\substack{j' \\ j' \neq j}} T_{ijj'} - \sum_{\substack{j \\ j \neq j'}} T_{ijj'}.$$

Equation (4) states that the amount of product i sold in region j, S_{ij}, cannot exceed the amount processed in the region, plus the amount shipped in, minus the amount shipped out, minus the amount exported, plus the amount imported.

$$(5) \quad E_i^* \geq \sum_j (EX)_{ij}.$$

---

4. Production activities can use primary products produced by other production activities, as well as produce primary products. For example, livestock activities use feed produced by crop activities; hence, b_{pjm} may be either positive or negative.

Equation (5) states that the amount of product i exported from all regions, j, must not exceed the upper bound or limit, E_i.

(6) $\quad I_i^* \geq \sum_j (IM)_{ij}.$

Equation (6) states that the amount of product i imported by all regions, j, must not exceed the upper bound or limit, I_i.

These import and export bounds are set to make the trade levels of the programming solution consistent with government trade policy or price conditions of world trade.

(7) $\quad S_{ij}, M_{mj}, P_{pj}, (IM)_{ij}, (EX)_{ij} T_{ijj'} \geq 0.$

Equation (7) is the standard linear programming constraint that states that all variables cannot be at negative levels.

In addition to these real constraints, there are $I \cdot J$ pseudo-constraints that are necessary to convert this nonlinear programming problem to a linear problem. The objective function is nonlinear because utility functions, λ_{ij}, are included in place of fixed prices for selling or consumption activities.

(8) $\quad K_{ij}^* \geq \sum_n k_{ijn}^* S_{ijn}.$

Equation (8) states that the weighted sum of product, i, sold in region j through all demand segments, n, cannot exceed K_{ij}, where K_{ij}/k_{ijn} is the maximum amount that can be sold through demand segment n. The upper bound, K_{ij}, would never be set above the amount for which total utility is a maximum. The range of n varies with the amount of precision desired in approximating the utility function.

The procedure may be elucidated by the following example. Given demand functions of the form:

(9) $\quad P_{ij} = a_{ij} - b_{ij} S_{ij},$

(where P_{ij} = the price of product i in region j; S_{ij} = the amount of product i consumed in region j; and a_{ij} and b_{ij} are constants); and assuming that:

$$P_{ij} = \frac{dU_{ij}}{dS_{ij}},$$

(where dU_{ij}/dS_{ij} = the marginal utility of consuming product i in region j),[5] total utility, U_{ij}, is obtained by integrating the demand function:

5. This is theoretically true if marginal utility of income is constant and equal to US$1.00.

(10) $U_{ij} = \int_s (a_{ij} - b_{ij} S_{ij}) \, dS_{ij}$ and

(11) $U_{ij} = a_{ij} S_{ij} - \dfrac{b_{ij}}{2} S^2_{ij}.$

For programming, equation (11) was approximated by segmenting the function for 10 ($n = 1, \ldots, 10$) discrete levels of S_{ij} and a convex constraint.

To illustrate, assume that:

(12) $U_{ij} = 100 \, Q_{ij} - 0.25 \, Q^2_{ij},$

then evaluating equation (4) for

$$Q_{ij} \ (1) = 20,$$
$$Q_{ij} \ (2) = 30,$$
$$Q_{ij} \ (3) = 40,$$
$$U_{ij} \ (1) = 1,900,$$
$$U_{ij} \ (2) = 2,775, \text{ and}$$
$$U_{ij} \ (3) = 3,600.$$

Moreover: $\lambda_{ij} = \dfrac{U_{ij}}{Q_{ij}};$

hence: $\lambda_{ij} \ (1) = 95,$
$$\lambda_{ij} \ (2) = 92.5, \text{ and}$$
$$\lambda_{ij} \ (3) = 90.$$

The coefficients of the convex constraint row are the following ratios:

$$\frac{K_{ij}}{S_{ijn}} = k_{ijn}$$

or $\dfrac{K_{ij}}{S_{ij(1)}} = \dfrac{40}{20} = 2,$

$$\frac{K_{ij}}{S_{ij(2)}} = \frac{40}{30} = \frac{4}{3}, \text{ and}$$

$$\frac{K_{ij}}{S_{ij(3)}} = \frac{40}{40} = 1.$$

Partial matrix

			90	92.5	95
Objective function		$=$	90	92.5	95
Supply row for S_{ij}	0	$\geq$	1	1	1
Convex constraint	40	$\geq$	1	4/3	2

Then by proper row and column divisions—that is, dividing the convex constraint row by 40 and then each column by the resulting coefficient in the convex constraint row—the matrix becomes:

			3600	2775	1900
Objective function		$=$	3600	2775	1900
Supply row for S_{ij}	0	$\geq$	40	30	20
Convex constraint	1	$\geq$	1	1	1

This form was used for programming because it is easily generated by the computer.

Finally, because the U_{ij} have a common constraint:

$$\Delta U_{ij}\,(1) = U_{ij}\,(1) - 0, \qquad \text{for } S_{ij}\,(1) - 0$$
$$\Delta U_{ij}\,(2) = U_{ij}\,(2) - U_{ij}\,(1), \qquad \text{for } S_{ij}\,(2) - S_{ij}\,(1)$$
$$U_{ij}\,(3) = U_{ij}\,(3) - U_{ij}\,(2), \qquad \text{for } S_{ij}\,(3) - S_{ij}\,(2),$$

hence, as $\Delta Q_{ij} \rightarrow d\,(S_{ij})$, $\Delta U_{ij} \rightarrow P_{ii}$.

PRIMAL AND DUAL SOLUTIONS

The theory of dualism in mathematical programming problems has been well explored and explained.[6] It is presented here briefly because of its relevance for data to be presented later.

The model can be depicted in compact form. The primal problem is:

Maximize

$$w = rx;$$

subject to

$$Ax \leq b$$

and

$$x \geq 0,$$

6. See, for example, Robert Dorfman, Paul A. Samuelson, and Robert Solow, *Linear Programming and Economic Analysis* (New York: McGraw-Hill, 1958), pp. 100–04.

Figure 2. Partial Schematic of Structure of the Linear Programming Model

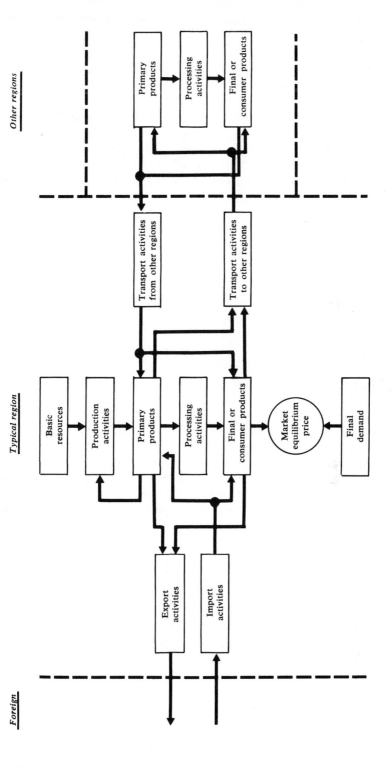

where w is a scalar of total net social payoff; r is a row vector of functionals (or social payoffs);[7] unit costs for production, processing, and transport; and unit prices for imports and exports; x is a column vector of activity levels for final consumption, production processing, transport, imports, and exports; and A is an input-output coefficient matrix for production, processing, and nonagricultural resources. Each function, variable, and parameter in the model has a spatial label: for example, consumption of wheat in region 1 and consumption of wheat in region 2.

The dual problem then is:

Minimize

$$m = ub$$

subject to

$$A'u' \geq r',$$
$$u \geq 0,$$

where m is a scalar of total value of resources; u is a row vector of shadow prices for the corresponding resources (column vector b); and $'$ indicates the transposition of a vector or matrix. The shadow price, u_i, represents the marginal increment (decrement) in the primal objective function resulting from a unit increase or decrease in the resource b_i.

Shadow prices that will be used in later analysis provide important criteria for investment planning. It pays to invest in—that is, increase the level of—a resource only if its shadow price is greater than its cost, even minutely. Shadow prices are somewhat analogous to marginal profits. But, because of discontinuities in linear programming problems, a shadow price may remain the same for only a small change in the related resource. On the other hand, it may not change when the related resource increases by from 10 to 20 percent or more.

EMPIRICAL STRUCTURE AND SOURCES OF DATA

In this section we present the sources, types, and method of data assembly, as well as the specific structure of the models. The results are presented in chapter 3.

---

7. Here social payoff is defined as the area under the demand curve which is a function of the level of income.

The 1968 validation model

Considerable time and resources were required to assemble data for the various analyses. The process began with the division of Portugal into regions for programming.

DELINEATION OF PROGRAMMING REGIONS. To minimize the size of the linear programming matrix—since all the agricultural products of Portugal would be included in the analysis—the programming regions were selected under the general constraint that the total number of such regions should range between ten and fifteen.

Preliminary boundaries were drawn for eleven regions by using soil type and topographic maps and by an analysis of fifteen years of historical data on the proportions and trends of crops produced and on the trends and productivity of livestock enterprises for each of Portugal's 273 *concelhos* (counties). These preliminary regions were reviewed by the Center for Agricultural Economic Studies of the Gulbenkian Foundation in Lisbon, and some of the boundaries were redrawn. The final boundaries are shown in the map on the facing page.

BASIC RESOURCE CONSTRAINTS (R_{jr}). The specific resources constrained in the model were, first, land, subdivided into class A irrigated and class A nonirrigated land, as well as orange groves, olive groves, and other land; second, labor; third, animal power; fourth, tractor power; fifth, processing plants; and, sixth, fertilizer plants.

For land, all technical coefficients are expressed on the basis of a hectare. Each crop production activity is tied to a specific type or class of land.

Estimates of land resources were based on data from the 1968 Census of Agriculture, which includes information on total use by crops and the amount irrigated. Class A land represents the top three land capability classes in Portugal and encompasses about 10 percent of all agricultural land, including irrigated land.

Labor required for cultivation and livestock production activities is expressed in man-hours. Labor use was constrained by its availability in each calendar quarter. For the base period 1968, labor availability was estimated by interpolating the two latest census years, 1960 and 1970. Because 1970 census summaries are available only by district, it was necessary to use 1960 *concelho* data to allocate the district labor force to regions when the regional boundaries were different from the district boundaries.

Labor was expressed in adult male equivalent man-hours, using the following coefficients: males 16–65 years of age, 1.00 unit; females

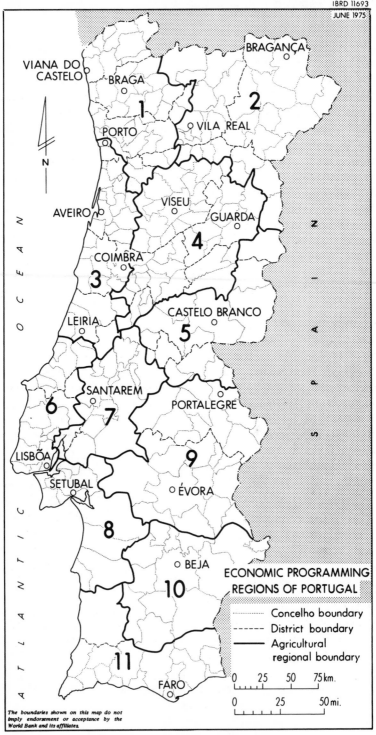

ECONOMIC PROGRAMMING
REGIONS OF PORTUGAL

.... Concelho boundary
– – – – – District boundary
———— Agricultural
          regional boundary

0   25   50   75 km.

0   25   50 mi.

16–65, 0.75 unit; males 12–16, 0.75 unit; and females 12–16, 0.375 unit. Further, the farm work week was assumed to be forty-five hours, or five days at nine hours a day.

Animal draft power, still a significant agricultural resource in Portugal, was estimated based on livestock inventory recorded in the 1968 Census of Agriculture. Animal power was constrained by its estimated availability in each quarter. In Portugal four types of animals are used as sources of draft power: mules, bulls, milk cows, and beef cows. Animal power was standardized on the basis of its relative productivity, which was determined by availability for work, size, and speed. Based on these criteria, the standard weights were work bulls, 1.00 units; mules, 0.82 unit; beef work cows, 0.48 unit; and milk work cows, 0.23 unit. It was assumed that each standard animal unit would be capable of working 2,500 hours a year, or 625 hours a quarter.

Tractor power was constrained on the basis of tractor inventories recorded in the 1968 Census of Agriculture. Tractor power was expressed in terms of hours and total hours specified for each quarter. Tractor hours were all standardized in 40-horsepower tractor-equivalent units, assuming that the standard tractor could be used up to 1,200 hours a year.

Six types of processing capacity constraints were included in the model: slaughter capacity for cattle, for hogs, and for sheep; processing plants for milk and for cheese and butter; and storage capacity for meat. Processing capacity for wool was not considered a constraint.

The data on processing capacities for livestock and livestock products were obtained from the Junta do Pecuarios (Livestock Council), which had a special census tabulated in support of its own study of slaughterhouse requirements in Portugal. Cold storage of meat was constrained on the basis of cumulative slaughter and consumption patterns; all other processing capacities were constrained by maximum tonnage during the critical months. At present, each *concelho* in Portugal is required by law to have its own slaughterhouse and processing plants.

Use of nitrogen and phosphorous fertilizer was constrained by existing production capacity. Portugal, however, has no potash fertilizer plants, and it all must be imported. Imported potash was assumed to be brought into the country through the ports of Lisbon and Porto. Regions without their own fertilizer plants were assumed to be supplied through transport. All fertilizer plant capacities were expressed in nutrient tons a year.

CROP PRODUCTION ACTIVITY (P_{pj}): STRUCTURE IN THE MODEL. Because activities are the heart of the model, they must accurately reflect the structures and data of the economic process that they represent; otherwise, the results of the analysis will be poor. All crop production activities were specified in terms of one hectare and on a one-year basis. In most cases each hectare was assumed to produce several crops, depending on cropping patterns. For example, when a typical rotation produced maize and wheat, the outputs of the activity were the yield of 0.5 hectare of maize and 0.5 hectare of wheat. Only production activities for grapes, oranges, and olives were considered as nonrotational, even though the general practice may have been to produce other crops between the rows in some areas. This apparent contradiction was handled by accounting for the land between rows of grapes or trees as part of the land base for other crops.

Crop rotations or single-crop activities were differentiated by type of land and system of production used. The former comprised class A irrigated, class A nonirrigated, or other land; the latter, tractor power only, tractor and animal power, animal power only.

Thus, each crop could be represented at the most by nine possible activities, but in practice this was not the case, because certain combinations of these alternatives were not feasible. For example, rice production and therefore all related activities always require irrigated land.

The primary crop products produced by rotation were wheat, maize, rice, rye, barley, oats, dry beans, broad beans, chick-peas, potatoes, tomatoes, and forage; the primary nonrotation crops were grapes, olives, and oranges. These fifteen crops were the most important in Portugal, although sunflower and safflower were included in the 1980 model.

CROP PRODUCTION ACTIVITY: INPUTS. Although analytically desirable, certain inputs were not included in the cropping activities, because of lack of data or because they were insignificant.

Land related activities for crops were normalized on a per hectare basis. The six classes of land are listed above.

Labor inputs were differentiated by the four seasons of the year or the standard annual quarters: January–March, April–June, July–September, and October–December. These groups fit the critical periods of labor in the country quite well. To have specified labor requirements by months or lesser units would have been desirable, but this procedure would have expanded the matrix size greatly, yet probably would have added little precision to the results.

Tractor power and machinery coefficients were used as a proxy for other combinations of machinery input. In other words, tractor power represented a bundle of machineries. As long as these were a fixed bundle, or set, the results would not be distorted. (Also, it is common practice to purchase a set of machinery such as plow, harrow, planter, harvester, and so on.) As noted above, one type of crop activity included both the tractor and animal power. Estimated hours of tractor use per rotation included time spent on tillage, harvesting, and hauling operations, the last including the time spent to haul the produce to the village market or central feeding location for livestock. Operating costs for tractors and machinery, such as for fuel, oil, and repair, were included in the objective function. These costs represent only those items purchased from the nonagricultural sectors. These coefficients were derived from special studies conducted by the staff of the Center for Agricultural Economic Studies of the Gulbenkian Foundation.

Animal power inputs were expressed in female units and handled in a manner similar to tractors. No explicit costs were attached to the cropping activity for animal power. Most relevant costs were accounted for through human labor and feed inputs (directly or indirectly) that were required to sustain and maintain work animals. Because it was not possible to obtain satisfactory cost information on veterinarian services and medicines, these were not included as costs.

Levels of fertilizer application used for crop activities were those used by average farmers employing the rotations considered. Costs of fertilizer inputs were set at the fixed government prices and included in the objective function.

LIVESTOCK PRODUCTION ACTIVITY (P_{pj}): STRUCTURE IN THE MODEL. Realistic livestock production activities are somewhat more difficult than crop activities to conceptualize and construct because of their long-term reproductive nature. All livestock activities, except that of mules and bulls (which produced only animal power), were based on the livestock production unit, with the female as the base. Each livestock production unit, or activity, included a female; a bull; replacement stock, both male and female; and male and female stock for slaughter. These were expressed in the proportion found in the average herd. Thus, a typical livestock production unit might include the following: one adult female, one-tenth adult male, one-third female calf, one-third male calf, one-third yearling female, and one-sixth yearling male.

The livestock production activities were animal power (mules and bulls), beef cattle, dairy cattle, swine, and sheep. These production activities produced the following primary products: beef cattle and calves, swine, sheep and lambs, wool, sheep milk, and cow milk.

LIVESTOCK PRODUCTION ACTIVITY: INPUTS. Labor inputs, as with crop activities, were defined by quarters. Both crop and livestock labor was drawn from the same labor pools or constraints. Thus, all labor was presumed to have the necessary skills for both crop and livestock production.

Three classes of feed inputs were specified: forage from grass, hay, and silage, and high-protein and low-protein concentrates. These were expressed in standard European feed units, or UFs. The low-protein concentrates were from the feed grains of maize, oats, or barley; high-protein concentrates were from soybeans, peanuts, or cottonseed, all of which were considered imported.

STRUCTURE OF MARKETS. The final demand for agricultural products was measured in retail prices for several reasons. First, and most practical, it was only at the retail, or final consumer, level that a full set of prices for agricultural commodities was available. Second, we wanted to look at constraints on development that were related to processing facilities. This was particularly true for livestock products, since there has been much discussion in Portugal about the shortage of processing facilities as being the greatest constraint on an increase of livestock production.

PROCESSING ACTIVITIES (M_{mj}). Because many products were consumed in different forms—that is, raw, canned, or in some other form—processing activities represented composites of the several different transformations involved. The cost associated with these activities included not only that of processing but also that of handling and other marketing margins—except transport, which was treated separately. Most of the processing activities use or consume the processing facilities and thus cannot exceed the level of the related processing capacity (see equation [2]).

DOMESTIC DEMAND FOR AGRICULTURAL PRODUCTS. Much effort went into the study of retail demand for farm products. The first step was to estimate demand functions of the form:

$$P_{ij} = \int (S_{ij}, I_j),$$

where S_{ij} = per capita consumption of commodity i in jth region; P_{ij} = price of commodity i in the jth region; and I_j = per capita income in the jth region.

It would have been desirable to include prices of other substitutable commodities in this function. Food prices, however, tend to be highly collinear, a fact that does not permit statistical estimation of cross elasticities for invidual commodities. Lack of regional data on consumption presented a serious problem in estimating regional demands. A first attempt was made by estimating demand functions for each commodity at the national level. These functions were then used to estimate quantities consumed, region by region, on the basis of per capita incomes and prices. The resulting consumption patterns were then compared on the basis of a priori expectations. These did not turn out well. Consequently, a second allocation of regional consumption patterns was made on the basis of per capita local production of crops and livestock products. Thus, a typical per capita yearly food ration was derived for each region. These were examined in terms of average consumption—by weight and by calorie and protein intake per person—in relation to the regional per capita income. When any of these criteria seemed improbable, national totals were reallocated to move regional consumption rates into a plausible range.

After these analyses we needed some formal expression of regional demand. Therefore, we analyzed (or fit demand functions to) regional consumption patterns on the assumption that, given the present patterns of consumption, the price and income elasticities were the same in all regions. This was not very satisfactory, of course, but under the circumstances it seemed to be the most practical course.

Demand functions were estimated for the following products: wheat flour, maize products, milled rice, rye products, barley products, oat products, dry beans, broad beans, chick-peas, potatoes, tomato paste, wine, olive oil, oranges, beef and veal, pork, bacon, and lard, lamb and mutton, fresh milk, cheese, butter and wool.

Lack of historical data made it impossible to obtain regional demand functions in terms of regional price and income for all products that were included in the analysis. Powdered skim milk, wool, and tomato products were not represented by regional demand functions, but a national demand function for wool was derived by using data for Lisbon, assuming that all wool was transported to that city for sale. For tomato products, only export demand was considered; these were priced for export at 7.75 escudos a kilogram, with the quantity in upper limit, or bound, of 138,000 metric tons. Powdered skim milk was assumed to be sold at 20 escudos a kilogram, with no limit on consumption at this price. These same demand functions were also used for the 1980 analysis.

As noted before, for programming purposes, and because a linear algorithm was used, the equilibrium demand (supply price equal to demand price) was approximated by using segmented demand functions. The supply-demand market equilibrium can be approximated as near as desired by increasing the number of segments.

Figure 3 shows the demand-supply situation for both historic and one programming result. DD_1 represents the segmented demand curve for

Figure 3. Market Equilibrium of Oranges in Region 6

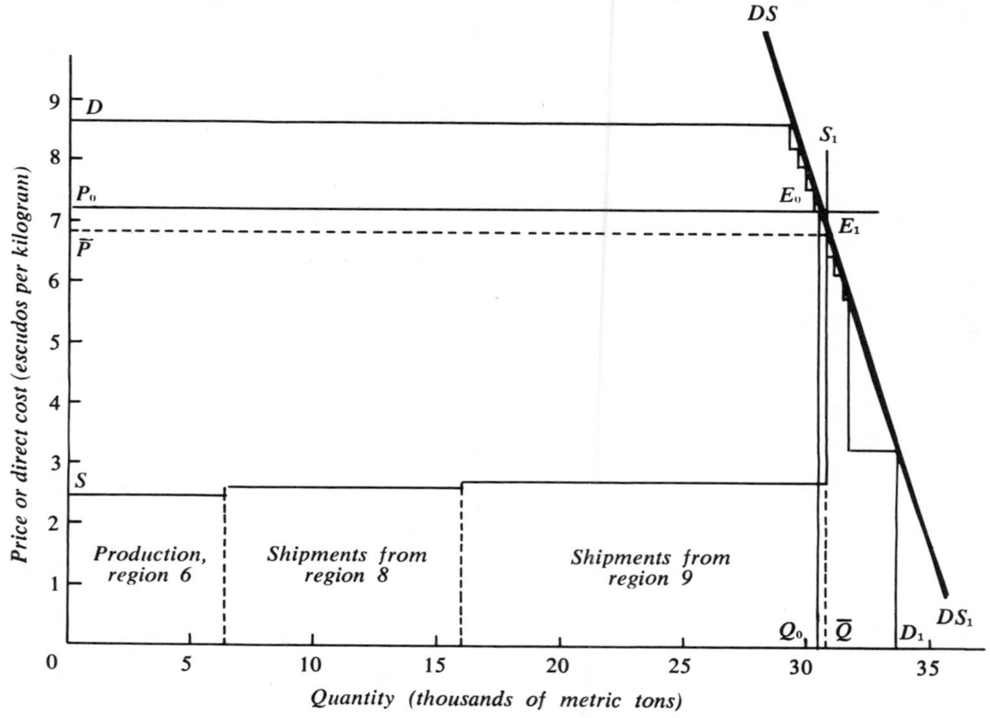

oranges. $DSDS_1$ represents the conventional demand function from which DD_1 was derived. (SS_1 is the postprogramming step supply function.) At the base price P_0, the consumption level is Q_0. The solution internally generates a stepwise supply curve, which incorporates the regional production, shipments from region 8, and additional shipments from region 9, resulting in the new equilibrium condition, E_1, at the price $\bar{P}$ and quantity $\bar{Q}$. The implication is that orange consumption in region 6 is relatively high enough so that, even bearing the transport cost, it pays economically to import from other regions. As a result, the new equilibrium supply has become larger at a lower price.

EXTERNAL TRADE $[(EX)_{ij}, (IM)_{ij}]$. Only traditionally traded commodities were represented by import or export activities, because aggregate analyses demonstrated that under the current situation of production and demand only a few commodities offer real potential for export growth. Products with export possibility were wine, olive oil, lamb (for special markets in Europe), and the newly developed tomato products. On the import side, beef, pork, wheat, rice, maize, and feed concentrates appeared to have the greatest potential. Products were not included that were not produced in Portugal: cotton, sugar, tobacco, for example, that were by law the special domain of the overseas provinces. Though it would have been desirable to have export demand functions and import supply functions such as those derived for internal markets, these could not be estimated from available data. It was difficult to obtain relevant export and import prices. For most agricultural imports—wheat, maize, feed concentrates, beef, and pork—it is quite realistic to assume that the supplies available to Portugal were infinitely elastic. This, however, is not the case for exports of wine, olive oil, and tomatoes. To ensure that exports would not be greater than could be marketed at the assumed export prices, an upper limit was placed on each of these exports. Moreover, to simulate the market structure in 1968, import constraints were also imposed on wheat, beef, and pork.

TRANSPORT ACTIVITIES (T_{ijj}). It was assumed that, consistent with conditions in Portugal, agricultural products would in most cases be transported in raw form and then processed in the region in which they were to be consumed. Most of the raw milk is taken to or near the large urban areas around Lisbon or Porto for processing and is consumed there.

Cheese and butter are assumed to be transported between all regions, and pasteurized milk from region 6 to regions 7 and 8 and from region 3 to regions 1 and 4. This structure was used because it also represented the actual market situation.

Most of the transport activities assumed that the hauling would be done by truck. The cost for this type of conveyance was based on a study by German consultants.[8] Transport of grains and fertilizer, which received special rates, was assumed to be by rail, since the time element was not very important in the transfer of these products, and in most instances railroads actually are used.

Simplified models

Models of the type outlined above require tremendous amounts of data, manpower, and computer services. Consequently, the question of using simpler formulations is important. We investigated two alternative approaches to the size problem. In one case, only two regions were programmed out of the eleven; and in the other case, the eleven regions were aggregated into three. We briefly describe the structure of the simplified models here. The results are presented in chapter 4.

THE TWO-REGION PARTIAL MODEL. To program the two-region partial model, it was necessary to make some assumptions about "rest of the world." These included assumptions, first, about the commodities that could be imported from, and exported to, other countries of the world, together with their prices and maximum quantities; and, second, about the commodities that could be imported from, and exported to, other regions within the country, together with their prices.

Regions 1 and 2, both in the northern part of the country (see Figure 3), were selected for the partial model. Region 1 has a high population density and is usually a net importer of agricultural commodities, whereas region 2 is mainly an agricultural area and a net exporter of agricultural commodities.

Because import supply and export demand functions (with respect to price) were not available, it was necessary to specify fixed prices and to place upper limits on some foreign exports and imports. No limits were placed on imports and exports to other regions in Portugal. The specific assumptions used are given in Table 1.

THE THREE-REGION AGGREGATE MODEL. To shed some light on the question of possible bias in results in models with large regions, the eleven regions of the basic model were aggregated into three regions. One of these three regions encompassed exactly the same area and resource and activity set as region 11 in the eleven-region model. The main

8. Planungsgruppe Ritter, *Portugal, Reseau National des Abbatoirs,* 6 vols. (Konigstun: Allemage, October 1968).

Table 1. Assumed Exogenous Values for the Two-region Model

	Price (escudos per kilogram or liter)		Upper joint limit (thousands of metric tons or liters)
Product	Region 1	Region 2	
Foreign imports			
Wheat	3.36	3.45	77
Rice	6.33	6.42	16
Maize	1.92	2.01	. . .
Beef	17.09	17.22	1
Pork	22.42	22.55	8
Foreign exports			
Wine	5.61	5.48	136
Olive oil	14.04	21.41	3.7
Regional imports	*Both regions*		
Beans	6.82		
Chick-peas	8.43		
Olive oil	18.95		
Oranges	8.22		
Rice	6.57		
Wool	29.00		
Regional exports			
Rye	2.47		
Potatoes	1.28		
Lamb and mutton	26.00		
Milk	2.50		
Maize	1.50		
Cheese	46.00		

reason for not aggregating region 11 with other regions was to determine whether detailed analysis of a specific region could be carried out in conjunction with the rest of world analysis and produce more or less the same results as a full model with many (here, eleven) regions. A lesser but more practical reason was that region 11, because of its physical and climatic resource base, could not logically be aggregated with any other contiguous region. The eleven regions were aggregated as follows: regions 1, 2, 3, and 4 were aggregated into macroregion 1; regions 5, 6, 7, 8, 9, and 10, into macroregion 2; while region 11 alone made up macroregion 3.

METHOD OF AGGREGATION. Unfortunately, there are no clearcut rules for aggregating regions, production and processing activities, or demand functions in complex programming models of this type. As described below, we simply summed up or used weighted averages in most cases.[9]

Basic resource constraints—land, labor, and so on—were obtained for the macroregions simply by adding the resource levels of the microregions. Production activities were aggregated by weighting with estimated relative production levels in the 1968 base period. In a number of cases unique crop rotations were specified for the macroregions: that is, they were for a specific number of years and produced a unique mix of crops—unlike any other in the related microregions. In these cases no aggregating was done, and these activities had the same specifications as in the micromodel.

Transportation activities were aggregated by establishing new transportation points near the centers of the macroregions and recalculating transfer costs between these points, using the same basic rates per ton-mile as for the eleven regions.

Commodity demand functions were derived for the macromodel by computing new functions for each commodity using price elasticities, base period prices weighted by base period consumption, and base period total consumption in the regions aggregated. (Demand price elasticities were assumed to be the same for each commodity across all regions in the micromodel.) Micro demand function aggregated in this way would give an unbiased estimate of base period consumption and unbiased estimates of consumption if price changes within an aggregated region were proportional, as is demonstrated in the following section.

METHOD USED TO AGGREGATE REGIONAL DEMANDS. Given microregional demand functions:

(1) $Q_i = a_i + b_i P_i,$

where

$$b_i < 0,$$
$$b_i = e \frac{Q_{i0}}{P_{i0}}, \text{ and}$$
$$a_i = Q_{i0} - b_i P_{i0},$$

and where Q_{i0} and P_{i0} are the price and quantity in the base period in region i and e is the price elasticity of demand for a commodity (e is assumed constant over all regions).

The aggregate demand function was obtained as follows:

9. For convenience, the term "micro" refers hereafter to the eleven-region model, "macro" to the three-region model.

(2) $\bar{Q} = A + B\bar{P},$

where

$$\bar{P} = \frac{\Sigma Q_{i0} P_{i0}}{\Sigma Q_{i0}},$$

$$\bar{Q} = \Sigma Q_i \quad \text{and}$$

$$B = \Sigma b_i = \Sigma e \frac{Q_{i0}}{\bar{P}}; \quad \text{or}$$

$$B = e \frac{\Sigma Q_{i0}}{\bar{P}} = \frac{\Sigma b_i P_{i0}}{\frac{\Sigma Q_{i0} P_{i0}}{\Sigma Q_{i0}}} \quad \text{and}$$

$$A = \Sigma Q_i - B\bar{P} = \Sigma a_i; \quad \text{hence}$$

$$\bar{Q} = \Sigma a_i - \frac{\Sigma b_i P_{i0}}{\frac{\Sigma Q_{i0} P_{i0}}{\Sigma Q_{i0}}} \left[\frac{\Sigma Q_{i0} P_{i0}}{\Sigma Q_{i0}} \right].$$

Hence, if prices change proportionately from the base value in each region:

$$\Sigma Q_i = \bar{Q}.$$

If prices change by a constant, K, then:

(3) $\Sigma Q_i = \Sigma a_i - \Sigma b_i P_{i0} - \Sigma b_i K$ and

$$\bar{Q} = \Sigma a_i - \frac{\Sigma b_i P_{i0}}{\frac{\Sigma Q_{i0} P_{i0}}{\Sigma Q_{i0}}} \left[\frac{\Sigma Q_{i0} P_{i0}}{\Sigma Q_{i0}} + K \right]$$

(4) $\bar{Q} = \Sigma a_i - \Sigma b_i P_{i0} - \dfrac{\Sigma b_i P_{i0} K}{\bar{P}}.$

Comparing the last terms in equations (3) and (4):

$$K\Sigma b_i \quad \text{and} \quad \frac{\Sigma b_i P_{i0} K}{\bar{P}},$$

we see that the bias depends on the covariance of the b_i and P_{i0}. If the covariance is zero, $\Sigma b_i P_{i0} = n \bar{b} \bar{P}$, and there will be little or no bias. There is no strong reason to believe that b_i and P_{i0} will be correlated.

The development model for 1980

For the development analysis, 1980 was chosen as the reference year, mainly because it is a point in the future that would permit longer-term development plans to be implemented, as well as analysis of the relation between long-term needs and production possibilities. The development alternatives considered—which include irrigation, improvements in livestock herds, mechanization, and the use of high-yielding seeds, fertilizers, and insecticides—are standard ones requiring periods for both short- and long-term implementation.

Development analysis in a programming framework requires projections of the demands for agricultural products, domestic and foreign, and certain resources. In the framework used, the domestic demands for farm products were in the form of functions of population, per capita income, and prices. Because prices are endogenous in the model, essentially, projections are made of demand schedules based on population and income growth, rather than of a particular demand level.

POPULATION. The growth of population—or, in the case of Portugal, population decay—was projected using regional shifts in population that were reported in the official Censuses of Population for 1950, 1960, and 1970, as well as the nationwide trend. Even though the total country population was projected to decline slightly, in certain regions that include the large urban areas of Porto and Lisbon population was projected to increase because of the continued migration from rural areas.

INCOME AND DEMAND. Regional incomes appeared to differ greatly throughout the country, with the rural north at the low end of the scale and the Lisbon region being at the high end. Because of meager information on shifts in relative regional incomes, these were assumed to grow at the same rate as the total economy: 4 percent a year, or near the average rate of the 1960s.

Income elasticities used in projecting demand schedules for 1980 were derived from our studies of domestic demand for Portugal; they were slightly modified when necessary, based on studies of other countries, to reflect projected changes in income levels.

Several other new products were introduced in the 1980 model: first, some products—forestry, for example—were added to take into account real interdependencies in the rural areas and thus make the analysis more realistic; and, second, new products—in a commercial sense—were added to determine whether and how these could be fitted into the development picture. Products in the first category were melons, cork, resin, pine logs for lumber, for pulp, and for fiberboard, and eucalyptus logs for pulp; those in the second category were forage crops for milk cows, sunflower seed, safflower seed, oil from sunflower and safflower, and high-protein meals from sunflower and safflower.

For both sets of products, perfectly elastic demands were assumed at fixed prices, and in some cases an upper bound was placed on the amount that could be sold at this price. We note that demands for feed products were not required because they were implicit (derived) rather than explicit in the programming matrix.

LABOR FORCE. Among productive resources, only the projections of agricultural labor force were made. These, too, were based on the regional trends in agricultural population in the 1950s and 1960s. The accelerated rate of decline in the rural labor force of the 1960s was assumed to continue through the 1970s.

RESOURCES. It was assumed that inventories of traditional livestock, farm machinery, irrigation, and agricultural product processing and fertilizer plants would continue to be maintained at the 1968 base levels. Thus, to obtain net investment, any new investments that were put in place after 1968 must be subtracted from any programmed increase in investments required by 1980.

All projections and development analyses were made under the assumption of no changes in the price level. Thus, all the derived prices were in terms of 1968 constant prices. Relative prices for tradeable goods were projected to change somewhat from the 1968 base. These are presented in four unpublished statistical appendixes to this report.[10]

INVESTMENT ACTIVITIES. Each investment activity in the programming matrix represented a "package of investment goods." The farm machinery package included tractors, plows, and other tillage and harvesting equipment necessary to carry out specific types and rotations of crop production. Improved production activities for crops and livestocks were linked directly to the investment packages. Livestock investment packages included basic breeding stock, buildings, and equipment.

Activities for irrigation investment included the cost of building dams and the distribution system. The Department for Water Resource Development (Servicos Hidraulicos) in Portugal has had a plan since the mid-1950s to develop about 170,000 hectares for irrigation. Of this total about 100,000 hectares have been developed or are under construction. In the analysis of 1980 the remainder of this program provided the basis for analyzing whether development of the other 70,000 hectares should be undertaken on the basis of cost and benefits expected over the long-term life of the projects.

10. These four appendixes, nearly 450 pages in combined length, are entitled as follows: Volume I, "1968 Model Results"; Volume II, "1980 Model Results"; Volume III, "Basic Resources and Input-Output Data, 1968"; and Volume IV, "Basic Resources, 1980, and Input-Output Data for Improved Practices." A limited number are available from the Agriculture and Rural Development Department of the World Bank.

These possible irrigation schemes and their parameters are as follows:

Region	Irrigation scheme	Land area to be irrigated (hectares)	Estimated construction time (years)
1	Rio Lima	5,855	5
2	Vilariça	3,300	4
	Macedo de Cavaleiros	2,200	4
3	Mondego	14,930	8
4	Cova da Beira	17,000	8
9	Crato	6,500	5
	Vigia	1,220	3
	Minutos	1,800	3
10	Odivelas (two parts)	3,500	4
11	Odelouca	6,750	5

Forestry investment activities include costs of tree stock, land clearing, and labor for planting. Because some investment packages included items of different life expectations, and for irrigation all development expenditures could not be made in one year, all costs were expressed in present values. The life of the major investment in a package was taken as the life of the investment.

Moreover, because investments had to be related to annual returns for programming, and these investments had different life expectancies, the present value of each investment package was adjusted by a factor equal to the present value of an annuity of US$1.00. This procedure is explained below.

Given that the benefit cost ratio (BCR) is:

$$BCR = \frac{\sum_{i=1}^{n} \frac{R_i}{(1+r)^i}}{C_0 + \sum_{i=1}^{n} \frac{C_i}{(1+r)^i}},$$

where R_i is the annual return in year i to a project that has investment cost C_0 in period 0, and C_i is the annual operating cost; then, if $R_1 = R_2 = \ldots = R_n$ and $C_1 = C_2 = \ldots = C_n$, the above equation can be simplified to:

$$BCR = \frac{R \cdot S}{C_0 + CS},$$

where $S = \sum_{i=1}^{n} \frac{1}{(1+r)^i}$, or the present worth of US$1.00 payable for n periods. Hence:

$$BCR = \frac{R}{\dfrac{C_0}{S} + C}.$$

Therefore, the discounted annual benefit-cost ratio can be computed by dividing annual returns by the annual cost plus the investment cost divided by the present worth coefficient, S.

IMPROVED AND NEW PRODUCTION ACTIVITIES. Many farms in Portugal today follow traditional production practices which use large amounts of hand labor and animal power and employ, for the most part, simple tools. With mass migration of agricultural labor to the cities and the industrial countries of Europe, it is important to know what agricultural products will have the greatest economic advantage and what techniques should be used to produce them in the future. For this reason new production activities, in conjunction with investment activities, are introduced into the programming milieu for 1980. The input-output technical coefficients for these activities are based on the experience of the relatively few farmers who employ them and also on experimental results. Although it is not certain how many farmers could and would change to new methods within a short time span, results from the analysis provided economic goals that can be used for planning. And programs more conducive and effective than those used in Portugal today would have to be set up to encourage and assist farmers in their adoption.

3

Validation of the Model
Using 1968 Base Data

As for other models—statistical or by simultaneous equations or simulations—there is no prescribed systematic way to validate mathematical programming models. A good validation procedure depends to a certain extent on the use to be made of the model. Here we take the position that, for a model to be useful, it must be related in a logical degree to the current situation: in other words, the planner or planning agency must have some idea of his starting point, or base position. Moreover, the model must be consistent with the objective of that country and provide some guidelines for achieving that objective. Thus, the validation phase of the model must encompass both of these facts.

MODEL VARIANTS

Four alternative solutions are presented as examples of the validation process. A number of minor changes in the model were made before arriving at these. One of the most significant was extending the range of the demand function to be investigated and decreasing the size of the demand segments. The objective of this change was to obtain a solution—that is, a demand-supply equilibrium point—at an internal portion (within the range) of the demand function investigated.

It was also found by an earlier analysis that if exports were left unconstrained at historical prices, most of the products would be exported at levels much above their historical averages. Therefore, historical averages were used as upper constraints on all exports. It would have been more realistic to have had demand functions for exports as well as for domestic demand.

Other significant changes made were, first, addition of milk processing activities allowing for standardized butterfat content; second, addition of powdered-milk–processing activities; third, addition of high-protein feed import activities; fourth, separation of feed supplies into forages, high-protein feed concentrates, and low-protein feed concentrates; fifth, specification of two grades of olive oil for exports in place of one; sixth, addition of constraints for meat cold-storage capacity; and, seventh, addition of butter import activities.

The model variations to be presented are listed below, fully for variant A-1 and with reference to this list for variants A-2, A-3, and B. The results of these solutions are summarized to demonstrate the validity or nonvalidity of the model, as well as to show the type of economic information that is generated.

Variant A-1

Unique characteristics
Values in objective function include:
Utility as given by the demand function
Costs for:
Transportation
Fertilizer
Tractor operation
Processing
National constraints are considered on:
Exports of wine, olive oil, lamb, and tomatoes
Imports of wheat, maize, rice, beef, pork, and butter

Variant A-2 is the same as A-1 except that there are no constraints on imports of wheat, maize, rice, beef, and pork. Variant A-3 is the same as A-2 except that the value of imports cannot exceed the value of exports. Variant B is the same as A-3 except that fertilizer and tractor operation costs are not included in the objective function.

Variant A-1 is considered as the base solution because it includes constraints on imports of products that are controlled by government agencies. Thus, we expect the model solution based on variant A-1 to be closer to what actually occurred in 1968.

PRODUCTION

Regional programming models pay for their voracious appetites for data by generating mountainous streams of numbers in their solutions. Unfortunately, there is no simple way to summarize these results. Although summary statistics are available, these will be satisfying to some readers but not to others. Most of the summary tables are presented in the main text. Other detailed data are given in separate statistical appendixes that are available on request.[1]

The Theil U coefficient is generally used to summarize the correspondence between base data and the model output.[2] This statistic is superior to the ordinary correlation coefficient for the purpose. A comparison of programmed regional and realized regional production for variant A-1 shows that these data correspond better for some commodities than for others (see Table 2). In all variants, the correspondence of grape or wine production is exact—$U=0$—because the production is limited by the upper bound on vineyards. Except for wine and olive oil, which have specific acreage constraints, programmed production for livestock and livestock products correspond more closely with those of the base period than those for crops—which in general is also because of the fact that livestock production is constrained by base year livestock inventories, which are exhausted in most regions.

The correspondence between regional production and programmed production shifts among commodities as import restrictions on wheat, maize, beef, and pork are removed—the changes in moving from variant A-1 to variant A-2. The correspondence declines (and U increases) for wheat, rice, oats, chick-peas, potatoes, beef and veal, lamb and mutton, and cow milk. On the other hand, Us improve for rye, maize, barley,

1. See chapter 2, footnote 10.
2. The formula is:

$$U = \sqrt{\frac{\sum_n (P-A)^2}{\sum_n A^2}}$$

where P is the estimate or forecast, A is the actual value, and n is the number of observations. This coefficient measures how close each pair of observation falls with respect to a 45 degree line in a cartesian chart.

For a complete discussion of the nature and distribution of this coefficient, see H. Theil), *Economic Forecasts and Policy* (Amsterdam: North Holland, 1961).

Table 2. Theil *U* Coefficients, Comparing 1968 Normalized Regional Production and Programmed Production [a]

	Programming variant			
Commodity [b]	A-1	A-2	A-3	B
Wheat	0.26	0.43	0.42	0.40
Rye	0.33	0.26	0.25	0.28
Maize	0.25	0.21	0.23	0.19
Rice	0.52	0.54	0.54	0.52
Oats	0.45	0.76	0.76	0.75
Barley	0.55	0.42	0.42	0.34
Broad beans	0.47	0.32	0.32	0.27
Chick-peas	0.40	0.58	0.59	0.54
Potatoes	0.31	0.37	0.38	0.39
Dry beans	0.23	0.18	0.18	0.18
Olive oil	0.12	0.08	0.08	0.08
Wine	0.00	0.00	0.00	0.00
Beef and veal	0.17	0.19	0.19	0.17
Pork	0.03	0.03	0.03	0.03
Lamb and mutton	0.11	0.12	0.12	0.12
Cow milk	0.14	0.17	0.16	0.14
Sheep milk	0.30	0.27	0.27	0.27
Wool	0.20	0.16	0.16	0.16

a. A *U* coefficient of 0 indicates that the estimated values are equal to the observed values for all observations.

b. There are no official farm production data by regions for livestock and livestock products. The values used for comparisons were estimated fom livestock inventories together with national production.

broad beans, olive oil, sheep milk, and wool.[3] These shifts are not easy to explain. Part of the explanation is that the domestic wheat production is not competitive with imports at the assumed import price. Thus, wheat production declines and is replaced by maize and rye. Because crops are produced in rotation—usually chick-peas and oats are grown in rotation with wheat, and beans in rotation or interplanted with maize—these sets expand and contract together. Import restrictions on wheat raise its domestic price, making barley noncompetitive.

From these results, there becomes evident a great degree of effective interdependence in the model as it is structured intraregionally and inter-regionally. To a certain degree, "everything does depend on everything else," as in general equilibrium theory. But this interdependence is con-

3. There are no official regional data on the production of livestock productions, and comparisons are based on estimates derived from livestock inventories. Thus, they should be interpreted accordingly.

ditional and depends on the state of the solution and built-in discontinuities (or lack of substitution possibilities)—which results, at times, in small changes in certain variables that in turn lead to many changes in the solution or in large changes in certain variables that in turn lead to few changes in the solution.

In general, there is considerable stability in the solutions to the four variants. The pattern of wine production never changes, indicating that it is relatively more profitable than other commodities. Livestock production also is very stable, indicating high relative profitability.

In national production a comparison of actual production and programmed production commodity results in a lower U for variant A-1 than for the others (see Table 3). This result is expected because import

Table 3. Comparison of Normal and Programmed Production, All Regions
(Thousands of metric tons)

Commodity	Normal production [a]	Programming variant			
		A-1	A-2	A-3	B
Wheat	468.0	463.1	262.3	262.3	282.5
Rye	151.3	129.1	164.3	158.6	148.9
Maize	554.4	637.0	670.0	689.0	684.0
Rice	150.6	208.6	229.0	229.0	234.6
Barley	49.7	36.6	109.8	107.6	102.8
Oats	80.0	38.0	21.7	20.8	20.5
Broad beans	24.1	24.9	19.5	19.3	25.0
Chick-peas	21.6	10.2	8.9	7.7	7.8
Potatoes	924.0	906.0	906.0	906.0	906.0
Dry beans	48.0	45.1	52.7	52.3	53.6
Oranges	106.9	106.9	106.9	106.9	106.9
Olive oil [b]	63.6	55.6	59.2	59.2	59.2
Wine [b]	1,162.9	1,162.9	1,162.9	1,162.9	1,162.9
Beef	61.0	50.5	50.5	51.1	51.5
Pork	105.3	104.7	104.5	104.7	104.7
Lamb and mutton	27.3	23.4	25.2	24.9	25.1
Cow milk [b]	398.4	364.8	354.7	357.7	364.8
Sheep milk [b]	104.5	67.0	75.3	74.2	75.3
Wool	14.1	10.4	11.3	11.2	11.3
Theil U [c]		0.085	0.137	0.134	0.133

a. Normal production for crops was derived by multiplying time-trend yields by time-trend hectarages; both were estimated by least squares regression. Normal production for livestock was derived by multiplying 1968 cattle inventory by the long-range average of slaughter per female animal.
b. In thousands of liters.
c. A U coefficient of 0 indicates that the estimated values are equal to the observed values for all observations.

constraints simulate control of imports by government agencies. These controls affect domestic prices and relative profitability of domestic production.

CONSUMPTION

The correspondence between estimated and actual per capita consumption for some commodities, considering all the regions, is relatively good.[4] Wheat, maize, potatoes, beef, pork, and butter have a U value of less than 0.1 under variant A-1. The lowest correspondence is for chick-peas, the least economically important crop of those considered.

Shifts in the correspondence between the estimated and the actual consumption occur for each of the variants (see Table 4). However, variant A-1 produces the best correspondence on the average: the U values under A-1 are equal to, or less than, those for the other variants for wheat, maize, rice, broad beans, chick-peas, potatoes, oranges, wine, beef, pork, mutton, cheese, and butter.

The correspondence between total programmed consumption and actual levels is about the same for all variants (see Table 5). The pattern, however, is not the same for any variant, although A-2, A-3, and B yield the most similar results.

Finally, in the solutions some products are not programmed for consumption in certain regions. For example, for variant A-1 these are rice, in regions 10 and 11; broad beans, in region 1; chick-peas, in regions 5 and 7; dry beans, in regions 2, 10, and 11; oranges, in regions 4, 5, 7, and 10; wine, in regions 2 and 4; mutton, in region 2; milk, in regions 3 and 10; and cheese, in region 2.[5]

Only three regions, 6, 8, and 9, are programmed to consume some of each product. In the other regions, however, only one or two products are omitted from the diet basket. In general, these defects can be corrected by raising prices in the step demand functions. Unfortunately, time did not permit this to be done.

The relation of the programmed prices and the observed prices is

4. There are no official data on regional consumption in Portugal. Regional consumption patterns were estimated, as described in chapter 2.

5. Data are given in the statistical appendix, volume I (see chapter 2, footnote 10).

Table 4. Theil U **Coefficients Comparing 1968 Estimated Regional per Capita Consumption and Programmed per Capita Consumption** [a]

Commodity	Programming variant			
	A-1	A-2	A-3	B
Wheat	0.03	0.07	0.07	0.07
Rye	0.09	0.03	0.03	0.04
Maize	0.03	0.03	0.03	0.03
Rice	0.06	0.11	0.11	0.12
Barley	0.07	0.07	0.07	0.09
Broad beans	0.32	0.34	0.34	0.32
Chick-peas	0.44	0.57	0.65	0.64
Potatoes	0.05	0.05	0.05	0.05
Dry beans	0.28	0.24	0.25	0.23
Oranges	0.37	0.37	0.37	0.37
Olive oil	0.17	0.12	0.12	0.12
Wine	0.21	0.21	0.21	0.21
Beef	0.04	0.18	0.17	0.17
Pork	0.06	0.18	0.17	0.17
Mutton	0.16	0.16	0.16	0.16
Milk	0.27	0.26	0.26	0.25
Cheese	0.13	0.13	0.13	0.13
Butter	0.06	0.06	0.06	0.06

a. A U coefficient of 0 indicates that the estimated values are equal to the observed values for all observations.

similar to that for per capita consumption (see Table 6).[6] The U values are, under variant A-1, less than 0.1 for wheat, rice, barely, beef, pork, and butter, which are not quite as good as comparable figures for consumption. This poorer result is caused partly by price elasticities. With elasticities less than 1, large price changes result in small changes in consumption, and thus the U values are greater. Moreover, zero prices were assumed in regions in which no consumption was programmed; this may increase or decrease the relative correspondence, depending on the levels of prices and consumption. Comparison of national average prices and programmed average prices are given in Table 7.

U coefficients were also computed on a regional basis for per capita

6. In contrast to consumption data, commodity prices in Portugal are collected for the major regional markets.

Table 5. Comparison of Normal and Programmed Consumption, All Regions
(Thousands of metric tons)

Commodity	1968 normal	Programming variant			
		A-1	*A-2*	*A-3*	*B*
Wheat	580	545	664	664	664
Rye	118	98	124	121	113
Maize	225	238	239	238	239
Rice	131	146	160	160	164
Barley	17	2	2	2	2
Broad beans	35	25	19	19	25
Chick-peas	15	10	9	8	8
Potatoes	818	906	906	906	906
Dry beans	55	45	53	52	54
Oranges	120	107	107	107	107
Olive oil [a]	47	34	37	37	37
Wine [a]	1,042	788	788	788	788
Beef	76	71	109	110	110
Pork	98	108	143	138	139
Mutton	29	22	24	24	24
Milk [a]	322	193	201	201	211
Cheese	23	21	21	21	21
Butter	6	5	5	5	5
Theil U [b]		0.11	0.11	0.11	0.11

a. In thousands of liters.
b. A U coefficient of 0 indicates that the estimated values are equal to the observed values for all observations.

consumption and prices (see Tables 8 and 9). In per capita consumption region 9 seems to fare the best, with a U of about 0.05; regions 2 and 4 fare the worst, with U values between 0.25 and 0.30 (see Table 8); all other regions have Us near 0.1. The large U for region 4 appears to result from a lack of programmed wine consumption, which is unrealistic. On the price side region 2 again fares the worst, with a U of near 0.4 (see Table 9); all other regions have Us between 0.1 and 0.2. Comparisons within regions are just another way of looking at the performance of the model. These are not superior to commodity comparisons across regions, but a place to begin seems to be in regions in which programmed production and prices are not close to actual levels.

Table 6. Theil *U* Coefficients, Comparing 1968 Regional Retail Prices and Programmed Retail Prices [a]

Commodity	Programming variant			
	A-1	*A-2*	*A-3*	*B*
Wheat	0.08	0.27	0.27	0.27
Rye	0.19	0.05	0.05	0.14
Maize	0.11	0.11	0.10	0.11
Rice	0.04	0.09	0.09	0.10
Barley	0.07	0.07	0.06	0.08
Broad beans	0.19	0.23	0.23	0.19
Chick-peas	0.26	0.28	0.30	0.30
Potatoes	0.12	0.12	0.12	0.12
Dry beans	0.32	0.18	0.21	0.14
Oranges	0.47	0.47	0.47	0.47
Olive oil	0.27	0.22	0.22	0.22
Wine	0.21	0.21	0.21	0.21
Beef	0.05	0.27	0.27	0.27
Pork	0.04	0.19	0.16	0.17
Mutton	0.20	0.21	0.21	0.21
Milk	0.24	0.23	0.23	0.22
Cheese	0.14	0.14	0.14	0.14
Butter	0.05	0.05	0.05	0.05

a. A *U* coefficient of 0 indicates that the estimated values are equal to the observed values for all observations.

REGIONAL TRADE

Because there are no official data on interregional agricultural trade patterns, the performance of the model can be appraised only on the basis of reasonableness. Because of the volume of data produced—for eighteen commodities and eleven regions—commodity-by-commodity interregional flows cannot be shown here; thus, we shall review only regional imports and exports, ignoring the origins and destinations. Complete data show that trade is more likely to take place among proximate regions.

Some commodities are traded interregionally relative more than others (see Table 10). Some 70 percent of the production of oranges and rice are traded interregionally, which means about 30 percent is consumed

Table 7. Comparison of Normal and Programmed Prices, All Regions [a]
(Escudos per kilogram)

Commodity	1968 normal	Programming variant			
		A-1	*A-2*	*A-3*	*B*
Wheat	6.00	7.08	3.43	3.45	3.43
Rye	5.17	6.03	4.87	5.06	5.35
Maize	4.95	3.99	3.99	4.05	3.96
Rice	5.89	5.43	4.96	4.96	4.83
Barley	5.93	5.20	5.19	5.34	5.10
Broad beans	8.69	9.10	9.29	9.21	9.04
Chick-peas	8.20	10.12	10.12	10.96	10.91
Potatoes	1.85	1.46	1.46	1.46	1.46
Dry beans	9.67	10.87	9.44	9.40	9.39
Oranges	6.34	7.41	7.41	7.41	7.41
Olive oil [b]	15.73	22.10	20.11	20.11	20.11
Wine [b]	4.54	5.83	5.83	5.83	5.83
Beef	30.60	32.60	17.13	17.13	17.13
Pork	33.22	30.90	22.48	23.53	23.32
Mutton	32.50	40.54	38.83	39.26	38.83
Milk [b]	3.20	4.26	4.27	4.27	4.23
Cheese	56.10	61.43	61.43	61.43	61.43
Butter	42.37	46.70	46.70	46.70	46.70
Thiel U [c]		0.11	0.11	0.11	0.11

a. Prices are weighted by consumption of each commodity in each region.
b. In escudos per liter.
c. A U coefficient of 0 indicates that the estimated values are equal to the observed values for all observations.

in the region in which it is produced (none is imported or exported). On the other hand, all oats are consumed where they are produced. When imports of products are restricted (variant A-1), interregional trade tends to increase: for example, interregional trade of beef, pork, and wheat all increase when their imports are constrained.

Regions 2, 9, 10, and 11 are the largest exporters of agricultural commodities, as specified by the model solution (see Table 11), exporting almost the full range of commodlities. This is the natural consequence of the ratio of population to agricultural resources. In other words, these regions produce a surplus of food.

Similarly, most of the regional exports go to the regions with higher

Table 8. Theil *U* Coefficients Comparing 1968 per Capita Consumption and Programmed per Capita Consumption of All Commodities within Each Region [a]

Region	Programming variant			
	A-1	*A-2*	*A-3*	*B*
1	0.09	0.08	0.08	0.07
2	0.26	0.26	0.26	0.26
3	0.11	0.11	0.11	0.11
4	0.29	0.29	0.29	0.29
5	0.07	0.08	0.07	0.07
6	0.11	0.12	0.12	0.12
7	0.09	0.10	0.10	0.10
8	0.06	0.07	0.07	0.07
9	0.03	0.05	0.05	0.05
10	0.11	0.12	0.12	0.12
11	0.03	0.05	0.05	0.05

a. A *U* coefficient of 0 indicates that the estimated values are equal to the observed values for all observations.

Table 9. Theil *U* Coefficients Comparing 1968 Commodity Retail Prices and Programmed Retail Prices of All Commodities within Each Region [a]

Region	Programming variant			
	A-1	*A-2*	*A-3*	*B*
1	0.08	0.13	0.12	0.12
2	0.37	0.40	0.39	0.40
3	0.11	0.14	0.14	0.14
4	0.06	0.11	0.10	0.10
5	0.09	0.12	0.11	0.11
6	0.12	0.16	0.16	0.16
7	0.09	0.13	0.13	0.11
8	0.14	0.17	0.17	0.17
9	0.11	0.11	0.11	0.11
10	0.14	0.14	0.14	0.14
11	0.16	0.17	0.16	0.17

a. A *U* coefficient of 0 indicates that the estimated values are equal to the observed values for all observations.

Table 10. Percentage of Domestic Production Traded Interregionally, by Variant

Commodity	Programming variant			
	A-1	A-2	A-3	B
Wheat	37	13	12	13
Rye	49	50	45	56
Maize	23	30	33	31
Rice	74	75	75	70
Barley	24	39	40	27
Oats	0	0	0	0
Broad beans	56	56	57	54
Chick-peas	70	77	69	70
Potatoes	47	54	63	56
Dry beans	30	26	26	26
Oranges	69	70	70	70
Olive oil	28	31	31	31
Wine	16	16	16	16
Beef	24	18	21	20
Pork	33	25	26	25
Lamb and mutton	63	71	71	71
Cow milk	18	18	18	18

population concentrations: regions 1, 3, 6, and 8 (see Table 12). There is nothing surprising about these results: if they did not turn out this way, the analysis would be highly suspected because they would not coincide with our concepts of why and how interregional trade takes place.[7]

Another interesting sidelight to interregional trade is interregional balances of payments. These can be computed from the programming solutions, but there was no time to do this. In some development schemes there may be an interest in knowing the regional balances of payments, since they may be important for some planning systems. They are not very meaningful for just one sector, however, since other types of trade and investments can offset sectoral imbalances.

7. The principles of interregional trade do not differ from those of international trade. Mediums of exchange and the restricted flow of resources (especially labor) and products only complicate any analysis of world trade.

Table 11. Interregional Export of Commodities, by Region, Programming Variant A-1
(Metric tons)

Commodity	Exporting region											Total [a]
	1	2	3	4	5	6	7	8	9	10	11	
Wheat		64,528							47,540	52,505	8,724	173,297
Rye		21,873	22,431				3,136		14,861	402		62,704
Maize	39,601										109,810	149,412
Rice							37,300		80,908	37,725		155,934
Oats												
Barley								529		8,271	706	9,506
Broad beans	322							817	12,955			14,094
Chick-peas					323					6,711	97	7,131
Potatoes		326,436		34,612		41,864	26,464					429,425
Dry beans						2,270	1,347	3,199		575	6,148	13,540
Oranges				1,215	4,672		8,547	9,764	14,722	11,766	24,099	74,785
Olive oil [b]		6,072		2,055	6,253					1,150		15,530
Wine [b]				88,513			95,229					183,743
Beef		3,008		3,295	1,790				1,738	833	1,334	11,998
Pork		617	13,980	3,729	550				7,279	5,262	3,217	34,835
Mutton	327	3,119		497	2,916		476	1,911	4,704	3,194		17,142
Milk [b]			44,888	3,027		9,970		5,681	1,697	682		65,944
Cheese	1,680	1,880			781				1,670	371		6,383
Butter					35					69		104

a. Items may not add to total because of rounding.
b. In thousands of liters.

Table 12. Interregional Import of Commodities, by Region, Programming Variant A-1
(Metric tons)

Commodity					Importing region							Total [a]
	1	2	3	4	5	6	7	8	9	10	11	
Wheat	10,123			54,405	8,497	61,972	31,057	7,240				173,297
Rye	12,935			10,975	9,001	29,139		653				62,704
Maize		4,719	39,601	34,387	13,532	25,116	18,341	14,421	2,585	1,429	1,774	149,412
Rice	13,716		36,556	5,486	2,101	69,909		21,672				155,934
Oats												
Barley	54		475	292		510	169	706	7,300			9,506
Broad beans		584	5,024	1,419	326	1,502				1,494	3,744	14,094
Chick-peas	696	906	289	787		1,804		119	2,531			7,131
Potatoes	171,861		170,559		34,700			16,385	16,335	11,518	8,066	429,425
Dry beans	2,925		3,892	3,038				3,149	535			13,540
Oranges	27,322	2,437	20,559			24,467						74,785
Olive oil [b]	6,698		7,682								1,150	15,330
Wine [b]			75,740		12,774				43,099	24,310	27,820	183,743
Beef	1,906		4,667			1,177	1,519	2,727				11,998
Pork	3,278					20,137	5,801	5,418				34,635
Mutton	1,417					10,865	818	3,082			51	17,142
Milk [b]		3,027	909			52,265		9,970			682	65,944
Cheese				366		4,843	231	592			350	6,383
Butter							35				69	104

a. Items may not add to total because of rounding.
b. In thousands of liters.

FOREIGN TRADE

As noted earlier, Portugal's agricultural trade balance has been declining rapidly in recent years. Many of the country's agricultural development programs have been aimed at increasing domestic production of food grains, feeds, and meat products in order to reduce imports. These imports are largely controlled to support domestic price policy for both producer and consumer.

Under variant A-1 import constraints were placed on wheat, maize, beef, pork, and butter, and export constraints on wine, olive oil, tomato products, and lamb. All of these were at their 1968 levels. In the solution to variant A-1 all of these constraints are met, indicating that, at the prices assumed (also for 1968), it would have been economically wise to import or export more of each of these products (see Table 13).

In variant A-2, all import constraints were removed, except that for butter, but the amounts imported of these unconstrained commodities did not increase in the solution. Imports of maize and high-protein feeds declined, indicating that a greater proportion of feed requirements was produced domestically. In solution A-2, domestic feed production increased, mainly on land that under solution A-1 was used to produce wheat. Imports of wheat are more than doubled in solution A-2. Even though imports of wheat, beef, and pork are higher, domestic production is not greatly depressed, and the larger total supplies result in higher domestic consumption—a point that has some implications for consumer welfare and will be taken up later.

Under variant A-3 exports were constrained in total but not individually, the constraint being the total value of exports. Because the total value of exports was almost as large as the value of imports for A-2, little change takes place in the import picture. Most imports decline slightly, but that of pork and high-protein feed increase. Variant B likewise shows little change in import pattern from A-2.

Exports in each variant do not change, remaining always at their upper bounds. This means in general that it would be economically feasible to increase exports of each of these commodities at their export prices (see Table 13).

RESOURCE USE AND SHADOW PRICES

An interesting and probably the most valuable aspect of the programming solutions for development is the levels of resources used and

Table 13. Comparison of Programmed Imports and Exports with 1968 Base Data

Commodity	1968 base data	Trade prices (escudos per kilo-gram or liter)	Programming variant			
			A-1	A-2	A-3	B
Imports (thousands of metric tons)						
Wheat [a]	174.5	3.33	174.5	454.0	442.0	437.8
Maize [a]	118.6	1.89	118.6	17.1	10.2	0.0
Beef [a]	20.4	17.00	20.4	59.3	58.7	58.3
Pork [a]	3.3	22.33	3.3	38.1	33.0	34.0
Butter [b]	3.5	15.42	3.5	3.5	3.5	3.5
High-protein food [c]	69.0	2.96	128.2	127.1	127.7	128.1
Potash fertilizer [c]	30.0	2.70	31.7	37.0	36.3	35.5
Total value (millions of escudos)	1,527		1,746	3,933	3,737	3,737
Exports						
Wine (millions of liters) [b]	375.3	5.70	375.3	375.3	375.3	375.3
Olive oil (millions of liters) [b]	21.9	21.50	21.9	21.9	21.9	21.9
Tomato products (thousands of metric tons) [b]	138.0	7.75	138.0	138.0	138.0	138.0
Lamb (thousands of metric tons) [b]	1.1	52.50	1.1	1.1	1.1	1.1
Total value (millions of escudos)	3,737		3,737	3,737	3,737	3,737

a. Constrained at upper bound equal to base data for variant A-1 only.
b. Constrained at upper bound equal to base data for all variants.
c. Unconstrained for all variants.

their shadow prices. Under linear programming duality, only exhausted or used-up resources have values or marginal returns (shadow price). Moreover, when shadow prices are multiplied by the levels of these resources used, their total value equals the net value of the product, which is the total value minus current production and distribution costs. Thus, shadow prices represent wages and rents to the fixed factors of production—and consequently incomes to the owners of these factors. Moreover, these shadow prices represent the marginal economic earning power of the fixed factors, which is useful information to have in project analysis.

With these points in mind, we review the results of some resource use and associated shadow price. Because of the volume of data, only the results for variant A-1 are presented; the results are quite similar for other variants.

In general, land and livestock inventory constraints are exhausted most frequently in every region. But one of the surprising results is that irrigated and class A land are not always used up to their limits (see Table 14). The reason is not clear, but a rather detailed region-by-region analysis indicates that an insufficient number of rotations are specified for these land resources: in other words, the model contains an insufficient variety of rotations. As a result, use of these special resources is constrained by declining prices of products that can be produced by them. This can be corrected easily by changing specifications for cropping activity.

In every region animal power is completely used, at least in one season of the year. Tractors are used in at least one season in all regions except region 5. On the other hand, labor is exhausted only in two quarters in region 7, indicating an underemployment of labor, but the labor supply may have been overestimated or the requirements underestimated. Still, the productivity of labor as specified in the model is much below that of other countries in Europe.

For labor and for tractor and animal power, the most demanding seasons are the spring and summer, when most planting and cultivating activities take place. But, during harvesting in the fall, labor again is in relatively short supply (see Table 14). Resource constraints are difficult to specify accurately, yet they have a great influence on model solutions. Factors such as labor and tractor and animal power are quite nebulous. Questions such as what the relevant work week is and how many hours a period can tractors and animals be realistically used have no easy answers. Consequently, final levels used in the models may be quite arbitrary. Sensitivity analysis can be used to look at the stability of shadow prices with changes in resource levels, although insensitivity of the solution to changes in resource levels is not always helpful. Lack of sensitivity in solutions may be the result of the total model design, which may not be realistic.

Some uses of land result in very large shadow prices. The shadow price for orange production reaches over 70,000 escudos (about $2,600) a hectare in some regions (see Table 15), and wine production also brings in a relatively high return to land. Livestock inventories also yield high returns according to the shadow prices. Livestock used as

Table 14. Percentage of Resource Capacity Used, Programming Variant A-1

Resource	Regions										
	1	2	3	4	5	6	7	8	9	10	11
Labor (hours)											
First quarter	33	81	35	48	43	58	100	96	36	38	37
Second quarter	75	56	75	78	75	36	56	4	19	44	45
Third quarter	60	90	52	41	68	52	100	79	47	51	50
Fourth quarter	59	57	42	34	55	24	33	42	41	40	31
Tractor power and machinery (hours)											
First quarter	23	25	25	20	4	53	20	0	26	21	51
Second quarter	100	76	100	100	9	68	62	67	67	31	99
Third quarter	47	100	71	100	35	100	81	100	100	100	100
Fourth quarter	53	8	15	10	3	51	100	25	35	21	32
Animal power and machinery (hours)											
First quarter	26	25	19	54	7	3	63	34	3	11	22
Second quarter	100	54	100	100	100	3	19	8	100	49	88
Third quarter	33	100	63	61	24	100	100	100	100	100	100
Fourth quarter	67	26	68	82	76	51	63	84	93	100	—[a]
Land (hectares per year)											
Irrigated	53	70	62	67	1	100	100	84	100	75	100
Other class A	—[a]	100	0	—[a]	—[a]	100	9	100	57	90	0
Olive trees	0	100	0	100	100	100	100	100	74	100	100
Vineyards	100	100	100	100	100	100	100	100	—[a]	—[a]	100
Orange trees	100	100	100	100	100	100	100	100	100	100	100
Other land	100	100	100	67	100	100	100	100	100	92	100
Livestock inventories (head per year)											
Mules	100	100	100	100	100	100	19	100	100	100	100
Bulls	100	100	100	100	100	100	100	100	100	100	100
Sheep	0	100	72	50	100	100	100	100	100	100	100
Hogs	100	100	100	100	100	100	100	100	100	100	100
Milk cows	75	100	100	100	100	100	100	100	100	100	100
Beef cows	0	100	0	100	100	100	49	42	0	100	100
Processing of livestock products (metric tons per year)											
Beef [b]	56	28	51	32	18	8	37	42	38	27	52
Pork [b]	100	72	64	53	86	30	42	29	73	73	67
Mutton and lamb [b]	100	0	100	44	0	49	100	100	100	100	100
Cow milk	40	0	0	—[a]	100	55	100	100	96	—[a]	—[a]
Butter and cheese	9	3	5	—[a]	100	4	83	—[a]	—[a]	—[a]	—[a]
Ewe milk	—[a]	0	—[a]	—[a]	—[a]	—[a]	—[a]	—[a]	—[a]	100	—[a]
Meat storage (escudos per metric ton)											
All meat	—[a]	87	89	—[a]	20	81	81	81	—[a]	—[a]	80

a. Not applicable.
b. Capacity in peak slaughter months.

Table 15. Shadow Prices of Basic Resources, by Region, Programming Variant A-1

Resource	Regions										
	1	2	3	4	5	6	7	8	9	10	11
Labor (escudos per hour)											
First quarter	0	0	0	0	0	0	29	0	0	0	0
Second quarter	0	0	0	0	0	0	0	0	0	0	0
Third quarter	0	0	0	0	0	0	42	0	0	0	0
Fourth quarter	0	0	0	0	0	0	0	0	0	0	0
Tractor (escudos per hour)											
First quarter	0	0	0	0	0	0	0	0	0	0	0
Second quarter	124	0	66	105	0	0	0	0	0	0	0
Third quarter	0	416	0	93	0	156	0	130	118	212	22
Fourth quarter	0	0	0	0	0	0	0	0	0	0	0
Animal power (escudos per hour)											
First quarter	0	0	0	0	0	0	0	0	0	0	0
Second quarter	37	0	24	33	55	0	0	0	11	0	0
Third quarter	0	200	0	0	0	80	76	19	1	25	8
Fourth quarter	0	0	0	0	0	0	0	0	0	2	0
Land (escudos per hectare)											
Irrigated	0	0	0	0	0	115	98	0	2,169	0	1,411
Other class A	—a	571	0	—a	—a	0	0	700	0	0	0
Olive trees	0	858	0	1,039	211	307	159	264	0	106	1,085

Vineyards	2,375	5,508	4,606	6,043	6,889	7,009	9,674	6,072	—[a]	0	5,986
Orange trees	69,737	74,591	45,103	54,385	43,687	62,813	57,453	43,886	67,074	72,032	70,504
Other land	89	437	101	—[a]	34	0	34	57	762	0	40
Livestock inventory (escudos per head)											
Mules	7,529	4,411	4,033	6,928	47	25,258	0	3,703	538	6,053	1,849
Bulls	8,882	7,059	5,461	8,859	2,048	32,592	1,457	5,805	1,291	8,229	4,320
Sheep	0	6,279	0	0	177	370	221	250	44	2	45
Hogs	10,807	5,693	8,784	9,912	5,213	11,892	9,863	12,826	10,458	11,404	11,842
Milk cows	0	6,279	2,494	1,535	6,889	7,995	5,317	5,747	2,428	334	9,020
Beef cows	0	3,656	0	1,407	2,407	10,537	0	0	0	0	4,120
Processing capacity (escudos per metric ton)											
Beef [b]	0	0	0	0	0	0	0	0	0	0	0
Pork [b]	333	0	0	0	0	0	0	0	0	0	0
Mutton and lamb [b]	533	0	13,637	0	0	0	238	238	8,579	6,512	23,874
Cow milk	0	—[a]	0	—[a]	—[a]	0	83	355	0	—[a]	—[a]
Buttered cheese	0	0	0	0	—[a]	0	0	—[a]	—[a]	—[a]	—[a]
Ewe milk	—[a]	—[a]	—[a]	—[a]	41,606	—[a]	—[a]	—[a]	—[a]	41,640	—[a]
Meat storage (escudos per metric ton)											
All meat	—[a]	0	0	6,068	0	0	0	0	—[a]	—[a]	0
Fertilizer (escudos per kilogram)											
Nitrogen	—[a]	—[a]	4	4	—[a]	0	—[a]	0	—[a]	—[a]	—[a]
Phosphorous	—[a]	—[a]	—[a]	—[a]	—[a]	217	—[a]	209	—[a]	—[a]	—[a]

a. Not applicable.
b. Capacity in peak slaughter months.

animal power give a high return in every region as do also swine or hogs.[8] Sheep, milk cows, and beef cows are not as profitable or as consistently profitable as swine over all regions. This lower profitability probably is caused by inefficiency of feed conversion by sheep, milk cows, and beef cows and by relatively lower prices for livestock products.

SECTORAL INCOME AND CONSUMER WELFARE

The type of sectoral model used for the study reported here produces some interesting welfare and income data that have an important bearing on sectoral economic policies. As can be seen in equation (1) in chapter 2, the model produces estimates of net payoffs (consumer and producer surpluses) and sectoral incomes that vary with production and consumption levels. The solution value of the function represents the total social value of all goods consumed minus the cost of providing the goods. Furthermore, if there are no restrictions on imports (in which case import prices are equal to domestic prices), derived market prices can be used to value consumption, and an estimate can be obtained of sectoral income or producer surplus. The function as it is shown gives the net social payoff or consumers' and producers' surplus. That is, it represents the total social value of all goods consumed (not the value at the margin) minus the cost of providing those goods. (If the selling prices are used to value products instead of social payoff, and if there are no restrictions on imports, the result would be sectoral income or producer surplus.)[9]

Agricultural income under variant A-1 totals 13.8 billion escudos. Under variant A-2 domestic farm and retail prices fall with larger imports and total income of producers declines by over 3.1 billion escudos. On the other hand, the net social payoff from the added consumption is 0.9 billion escudos. The loss of income to the agricultural sector represents a direct transfer of benefits to consumers. Thus, the total benefit to consumers that results from removing import constraints on wheat, maize, beef, and pork—that is, as is done in variant A-2—is 4.0 billion escudos.

---

8. These inventories represent a group, or set, of animals necessary to carry out the enterprises: males, replacements, and so on.

9. Constraints on imports may yield a c.i.f. (cost, insurance, and freight) and domestic price difference. In this case the windfall would probably accrue to traders with import licenses, not to farmers.

Figure 4. Changes in Producer and Consumer Surplus with Changing Import Policy

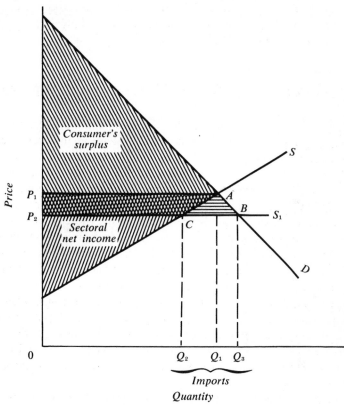

These changes are characterized roughly in Figure 4, in which aggregate supply and demand curves are presented. Triangle *ABC* represents 0.9 billion escudos in net social payoff derived from variant A-2, and trapezoid P_1P_2CA represents the 3.1 billion escudos of income transfer. Trapezoid P_1P_2BA represents total additional benefit to consumers.

This shifting of incomes with changing policies represents a type of dilemma faced often by policymakers. It is very difficult to opt for free trade when it has such an immediate and direct visible impact on a particular sector, which may be represented by a highly organized and vocal group, regardless of the total social benefits and welfare implications. Given certain price and income objectives, the easy way often is to control imports and exports rather than to effect income transfer programs. Nor is it easy to determine an equitable price level. Farmers view rising prices as just and consumers view them as exploitation. Moreover, a large part of the income of the agricultural sector represents rents and quasi-rents, which change dramatically with changes in supply because of the inelastic demand for food and of the nature of supply at the margin. (With respect to the latter point, a steeply rising supply at the margin produces high rents for intramarginal resources.)

It would be useful to evaluate the regional income in a way similar to that used above. Because both retail and producer prices and trade are endogenous in the model, however, such information is not directly available from the solution and must be computed by laborious secondary calculations.

CONCLUSIONS

In general we conclude that the model performs quite well—in fact, better than anticipated from a behavioral viewpoint. This is to say that the output of the model mirrors quite well what took place in 1968, so far as comparable data are available. These results imply (aside from import controls) that, given the fixed resources and technology employed, the producers, middlemen, and government made efficient allocation of production among commodities and markets. But the results do not imply that the fixed resources and technology set were efficient: if they did so imply, there would be no need for further planning analysis.

Because models of this nature and size require considerable manpower and resources, one major objective for this work is to determine whether and under what situations less complex models would give equivalent information on investment decisions. The next section summarizes and compares results of less complex models.

4

Simplified Models

The objective of these analyses was to determine how the results of a partial, two-region model and a three-region aggregated model (or macromodel) differed from those of the full eleven-region model (or micromodel).

PARTIAL MODEL

In Table 16 comparisons of the results are presented for the complete and partial models. Again, these comparisons are made in terms of the Theil inequality coefficient, U. As can be seen in the table, the results are mixed. If the historical base data are taken as the norm, for region 1 the U value is higher for production but lower for prices and consumption when all eleven regions are used to determine the solution than when just two regions are used.[1] On the other hand, for region 2 the Us are lower for production and prices but higher for consumption. If the eleven-region model data are taken as the norm (because it is an efficiency model), the relevant comparison is between the eleven-region model and the two-region model. The correspondence for this comparison is quite good, especially for prices in both regions and for consumption in region 1—but there is a large discrepancy for production in region 2. On balance, the eleven-region model performs better.

In summary, the objective of this brief analysis was to determine how well a partial model can perform relative to a more complete and complex model. The answer, though not categorical, is that the complete

1. The two regions are regions 1 and 2 in the total model (see the map on p. 22).

Table 16. Comparison of Production, Prices, and Consumption, by Theil U
Coefficient, for the Base Data, Full Model, and Partial Model,
Region 1 and Region 2 [a]

		Comparison of		
Item	Region	Base data and full model	Base data and partial model	Full model and partial model
Production	1	0.35	0.27	0.30
	2	1.14	1.95	0.70
Prices	1	0.14	0.16	0.11
	2	0.09	0.14	0.11
Consumption	1	0.17	0.22	0.11
	2	0.49	0.07	0.52

a. A U coefficient of 0 indicates that the estimated values are equal to the observed values for all observations. The formula is given in chapter 3, footnote 2.

model does slightly better, keeping in mind, of course, that there is no such thing as a complete model. As in all partial analysis, the results depend on the quality of the estimates of the exogenous variables. In this particular case, these variables are the limits set on imports and exports and the prices of commodities traded with other regions in the country. Because the estimates for the exogenous variables of the partial model differ from the endogenous solutions of the complete model, the solutions will differ.

THREE-REGION AGGREGATED MODEL (MACROMODEL)

The objective of this analysis was to determine how the programming specifications change when a larger set of economic data and relations was added up and represented by a smaller set. The frame of reference for adding these items is their location. Thus, we have added up related data if they pertained to specific geographical boundaries.

The U values for comparison of the results from the macromodel and micromodel are shown in Table 17. Roughly, the U coefficient of 0.06 for production in macroregion 1 means that there is an average difference of 6 percent between the production specifications for macroregion 1 and the sum of the production specifications of the eleven-region model for microregions 1, 2, 3, and 4. Thus, the correspondence between

Table 17. Correspondence between Results of the Micromodel and Macromodel by Theil U Coefficients, Supply and Disposition Items [a]

Item	Macroregions			Total, all regions
	1	2	3	
Supply				
Production	0.06	0.17	0.13	0.09
Regional imports	0.97	0.90	0.45	0.41
Foreign imports	0.38	0.54	0.01	0.46
Disposition				
Food consumption	0.20	0.13	0.19	0.15
Processing	0.37	0.04	0.00	0.04
Feed	0.03	0.17	0.03	0.08
Regional exports	0.67	0.90	0.24	0.41
Foreign exports	0.31	0.28	. . .	0.32

a. A U coefficient of 0 indicates that the estimated values are equal to the observed values for all observations. Computed by the formula given in chapter 3, footnote 2, for all commodities produced in each region.

this set of specifications is quite good. On the other hand, the U of 0.97 for regional imports of macroregion 1 indicates that the correspondence is poor.

The general conclusion to be obtained from this table is that errors are greatest for the trade specifications, both internal and foreign; and except for processing in macroregion 1, all of the U values for production, food consumption, processing, and feed use are less than 0.2, or not excessively large.

Another useful way of evaluating the results is by computing the average bias in the aggregative specifications, or determining whether on the average the macro estimates are either too large or too small. If the sum of the overestimates equals the sum of the underestimates, the bias is zero. This analysis indicates that the bias is negative for foreign imports and exports in regions 1 and 2 (see Table 18). In other words, both imports and exports are underestimated in the macromodel. The lower import specifications result from the fact that, because of aggregation, the potential of domestic production is higher (see below). Consequently, domestic costs are below import costs, resulting in lower imports. On the export side, demand aggregation gives an upward bias to domestic demand, domestic prices are higher, and exports in total consequently are less. (For differences in specific prices and consumption for each model, see Tables 19 and 20.)

Table 18. Bias in the Macromodel Specifications [a]
(Percent)

Item	Macroregions			Total, all regions
	1	2	3	
Supply				
Production	5	13	1	8
Regional imports	68	−28	44	21
Foreign imports	−19	−39	1	−24
Disposition				
Food consumption	10	13	−5	11
Processing	41	−2	0	3
Feed	3	14	0	7
Regional exports	16	72	−19	21
Foreign exports	−31	−29	...	−24

a. From $B = \left[\dfrac{\Sigma(0_1 - 0_2)}{\Sigma 0_2} \right] \cdot 100$, for all commodities in region, where $0_1 =$ macroestimate and $0_2 =$ microestimate.

The reasons for the large errors in regional imports and exports are not easily discernible. The biases are both positive and negative (see Table 18). The comparisons are made only on a net trade basis for the micromodel; that is, regional trade specified by the micromodel within the aggregated regions is omitted. Shipments to adjacent border microregions of the macroregions theoretically cost more in the macromodel, since they are assumed to move farther than they actually do. On the other hand, shipments to the extreme microregions of the macroregions cost less. We can say no more at this point than that the regional trade specifications are different in the two models.

The positive biases, production and consumption, result partly from a dissociation of specialized crop production activities from specialized inputs. For example, a region may have a better soil and climate for grape production than another. If this region is aggregated with a lower-productivity region whose production was not specified in the micromodel, the results of the macro analysis may include production in all microregions with production greater than that given by the micromodel.

Because there is a positive bias in production specifications, regional commodity prices are usually less for the macromodel than those of the micromodel (see Table 19). This domestic production bias—lower cost and higher output—makes imports less competitive and imports

Table 19. Comparison of Average Commodity Prices between the Eleven-region Micromodel and the Three-region Macromodel
(Escudos per kilogram or liter)

| | Macroregions | | | | | |
| | 1 | | 2 | | 3 | |
Commodity	Micro	Macro	Micro	Macro	Micro	Macro
Wheat	7.14	5.10	7.04	4.80	6.90	5.10
Rye	6.04	4.91	6.04	5.29	—ᵃ	—ᵃ
Maize	3.94	3.90	4.13	4.13	3.73	3.73
Barley	5.30	5.40	5.10	4.15	4.91	4.91
Rice	5.60	4.71	5.36	5.30	5.32	4.71
Beans	9.07	7.05	9.01	6.73	9.52	8.92
Chick-peas	9.59	7.24	9.38	6.83	9.49	6.80
Potatoes	1.44	1.35	1.50	1.45	1.65	1.55
String beans	10.93	9.09	10.53	8.61	—ᵃ	8.71
Oranges	7.16	—ᵇ	6.83	7.30	6.85	—ᵃ
Olive oil	18.96	—ᵇ	18.73	19.22	18.94	—ᵃ
Wine	5.34	5.53	5.36	5.57	5.48	5.74
Beef	32.30	31.60	32.96	31.27	32.20	30.80
Pork	30.64	30.37	31.08	31.41	30.72	30.72
Mutton	36.47	34.75	37.43	35.13	—ᵇ	—ᵇ
Cow milk	4.78	—ᵇ	4.08	3.67	3.90	3.73
Cheese	61.03	55.87	61.82	56.36	61.97	56.34
Butter	46.60	36.13	46.76	35.97	46.00	36.00

a. No consumption specified.
b. Equilibrium price not determined.

fall in the macromodel. It is difficult to ascertain why exports also decline.

In a number of instances the production specifications for certain items are identical for the two models. For example, pork production in macroregion 1 is the same for both models. This is the case because, first, the aggregated pork production activity was weighted by the swine inventory in each of the four microregions, and second, the production in each microregion was limited by total inventory. Consequently, the results must be the same. This is true as well for a number of other production specifications.

Differences in transport costs apparently have not had a great impact on the results. In each of the models intraregional transport costs are ignored. Regional transport cost is 432 million escudos in the micro-

Table 20. Comparison of Average per Capita Consumption, Eleven-region Micromodel and Three-region Macromodel
(Kilograms)

	Macroregions					
	1		2		3	
Commodity	Micro	Macro	Micro	Macro	Micro	Macro
Wheat	63.8	72.3	85.7	97.7	113.3	125.4
Rye	17.0	21.3	13.8	16.2	—[a]	—[a]
Maize	36.1	36.2	23.3	23.2	25.3	25.6
Barley	0.3	0.3	0.4	0.4	0.5	0.5
Rice	12.4	14.8	41.1	49.0	29.1	32.6
Beans	1.6[b]	3.2	4.0[b]	6.5	10.8	11.2
Chick-peas	0.8	1.0	1.6	3.2	1.7	2.0
Potatoes	119.5	122.3	88.3	89.3	81.4	83.2
String beans	8.0	9.4	1.9[b]	3.4	—[a]	1.6
Oranges	12.9[b]	15.1	11.5[b]	17.2	15.4	—[a]
Olive oil [c]	4.9[b]	5.4	2.5[b]	4.3	5.3	—[a]
Wine [c]	76.4[b]	103.0	112.3	123.2	112.1	109.8
Beef [d]	7.5	7.7	9.9	10.5	3.7	3.9
Pork [d]	8.7	8.8	18.9	18.7	6.5	6.5
Mutton [d]	0.8[b]	1.1	5.2[b]	5.9	2.9	5.3
Cow milk [c]	10.9[b]	27.5	38.7[b]	45.1	29.8	30.9
Cheese [e]	2.2[b]	2.5	2.9	3.1	2.4	2.5
Butter [e]	0.6[b]	0.7	0.7	1.0	0.3	0.4

a. No consumption specified.
b. No consumption was specified in at least one of the microregions in this group.
c. In liters.
d. Carcass weight.
e. Product weight.

model but only 155 million in the macro. Transport costs do not, however, make up a large part of the value of the output. Total value of domestic production at retail is about 16 billion escudos. Thus, accountable costs are 2 percent less in the macromodel with respect to the retail value and probably had little influence on differences in results. This loss of information could be partly corrected, however, by using intraregional transport activities based on a priori estimates of the average distance each commodity is shipped within each region. This would be a good practice for models with small regions as well as large, and the results would be more in line with national income accounting for the transport sector.

CONCLUSIONS

It is apparent from the results that simple aggregation procedures, as used in the experiment summarized here, can produce large errors in program specification. Thus, if such models are used for development planning serious mistakes could result.

Two sources of significant errors have been noted: first, aggregation can preclude regional specialization that is consistent with regional comparative advantage, and, second, production activities requiring unique (quality) resources, such as water, soil, climate, labor, and so on, may through averaging be specified at levels above resource availability.

Both factors are at work in the model as aggregated, and the specialized activity bias seems to be overriding because production is higher for most commodities in the macromodel. It is also possible that the absence of transport charges within a macroregion reduces cost sufficiently to permit a larger output before marginal cost equals marginal return. But because transport cost is a relatively small fraction of the retail price, transport costs probably are not an important explanation. This point could be examined by doing sensitivity analysis on transport costs. Even though transport costs are not as important in a small country such as Portugal, they would be important in large countries in which only a few regions can be handled in the analysis. But as noted above, a better procedure than omitting intraregional transport charges would be to make a priori estimates of average transportation cost for each commodity within each region.

An apparently simple way out of the problems of specific resource and regional comparative advantage in models with large regions is to group or stratify activities by intraregional location and unique resource needs. Thus, it is possible to tie specific activities to particular locations or resources in macroregions. The programming matrix would have the same number of resource constraints and the same number of production activities, but the number of processing, demand, and transport activities would be drastically reduced. For example, if a ten-region model with five resources, ten products, twenty production activities, and ten demand segments is reduced to five regions, the matrix will become less than one-fourth the size of that for ten regions.[2]

These suggestions are just as valid for regional programming models of industrial and other sectors as for agriculture. The principals are the same.

2. The formula is $M=[(p+[k+1]m)n+mn(n-1)]\cdot[(r+2m)n]$, where p is production activities, k is the number of demand segments, m is the number of products, and n is the number of resources.

5

Development Programs

The primary purpose of this study was to use the programming model to provide agricultural development plans for the future. For this analysis 1980 was chosen as the reference year: mainly, because it is a point in the future that would permit longer-term development plans to be implemented and to analyze the relation between long-term needs and production possibilities. The development alternatives considered are the standard ones requiring both short- and long-term implementation periods. These include irrigation, improvements in livestock herds, mechanization, and the use of fertilizers, insecticides, and high-yielding seeds.

To further investigate investment alternatives, three variants were programmed. Variant 1 was similar to 1968 variant A-1, incorporating modifications presented in the last few pages of Chapter II; variant 2 was the same as variant 1, except there are no upper bounds on cold-storage capacity for meat; and variant 3 was the same as variant 2, except there are no upper bounds on slaughter capacity for cattle, hogs, and sheep or on processing capacity for milk, cheese, and butter.

Variants 2 and 3 are investigated because the solution to variant 1 included very large shadow prices for these resources. In each case it would have been better to include investment activities in the matrix and let profitability determine whether an investment should be made, but data on the investment cost of these resources were not available. Hence, we used the second-best procedure of variants 2 and 3: that is, removing the constraints on specified resource levels. With the solutions to variants 2 and 3 (as will be demonstrated later) it is possible to determine the amount of resource required to yield a certain payoff (the incremental value of the objective function). This payoff can then be compared with rough estimates of investment cost or investment cost measured at a later time to determine whether the investment would be likely to yield an acceptable rate of return.

As in the other phases of this study, all of the regional details of production, prices, consumption, trade flows, and resources used cannot be presented because of the great volume. These data also are presented in the statistical appendixes.[1]

This section first summarizes the investment and development types of prescriptions coming out of the model. These prescriptions are of two types: those dealing with long-term investment expenditures and those dealing with improved methods of production. These two facets are interdependent: for example, certain crop rotations cannot be used unless there is an investment in machinery needed to carry them out. In the next part a summary of the production and distribution program that would take place under improved methods is presented. Finally, these prescriptions are related to, and compared with, those presented in the Bank's Agricultural Sector Survey Report.

INVESTMENT PROGRAMS

We discuss investment programs first because they provide the foundation for development programs. Discussions of the solutions obtained for variants 2 and 3 are contrasted to, and compared with, that obtained for variant 1.

Variant 1

Farm mechanization accounts for a major part—40 percent—of the investment expenditure prescribed by the variant 1 solution (see Table 21). Much of this investment would be concentrated in regions 1, 6, 7, and 10. The reasons for this investment pattern are quite complex. For example, in regions 1 and 10, investment in machinery is prescribed, even though both conventional tractors and other machinery are not used. This occurs because it permits the use of production techniques that are sufficiently superior to traditional methods to offset the investment cost. On the other hand, in regions 6 and 7 to say that investment in machinery is prescribed because labor and other sources of power are used up is more reasonable, and investment in these items is profitable. These points are illustrated by the shadow prices for exhausted resources (see Table 22). (Recall that additional investment would not be pro-

1. See chapter 2, footnote 10.

Table 21. Summary of Investment Activities in the 1980 Model, Variant 1

Resources						Regions							
	1	2	3	4	5	6	7	8	9	10	11	Total
Units supplied													
Farm mechanization (number of tractors) [a]	1,281.0					1,342.0	1,421.0		783.0	1,141.0	63.0	6,031.0
Milk cows (thousands) [b]	44.6					59.0			2.5		2.4	108.5
Beef cows (thousands)					14.5		33.9		47.8			96.2
Hogs (thousands)			3.7					0.4		11.9		16.0
Sheep (thousands)		93.4					179.4	160.4	253.0		130.5	816.7
Pine (thousands of hectares)				286.6								286.6
Eucalyptus (thousands of hectares)	89.6											89.6
Value (millions of escudos)													
Farm mechanization [c]	99.0					96.8	90.9		53.7	76.2	2.5	419.1
Milk cows	116.0					194.7			8.2		7.9	326.8
Beef cows					12.5		28.6		41.2			82.3
Hogs			4.9					0.5		15.5		20.9
Sheep		15.4					29.6	18.8	29.6		15.3	108.7
Pine				47.0								47.0
Eucalyptus	31.9											31.9
Total	246.9	15.4	4.9	47.0	12.5	291.5	149.1	19.3	132.7	91.7	25.7	1,036.7

a. In 50 horsepower tractor equivalent.
b. Units of female stock. Investment package includes other associate livestock, buildings, and equipment.
c. Includes cost of tractor and auxiliary equipment.

Table 22. Shadow Price of Resources in the 1980 Model, Variant 1

Resources					Regions						
	1	2	3	4	5	6	7	8	9	10	11
Labor (escudos per hour)											
First quarter	1.85	1.31		6.99	6.13	5.38	16.50	0.77	9.85	1.35	0.01
Second quarter			1.70		2.07						
Third quarter		0.72				9.30	6.87	5.77	6.55	2.66	1.27
Fourth quarter		17.77									
Tractor (escudos per hour)											
First quarter			60.28								
Second quarter											
Third quarter						2.73	53.22				
Fourth quarter					17.61						
Animal power (escudos per hour)											
First quarter	2.13										
Second quarter		1.86	3.68	5.25	2.29			0.69		2.01	
Third quarter			2.70			3.80			1.80	0.04	1.65
Fourth quarter	1.12							0.88		0.02	
Livestock inventory (escudos per head)											
Mules			723	469							756
Bulls		419	791	814	696	456		23	247		539
Beef cows					119						
Milk cows		854			1,193	61	725	1,102	584	656	1,979
Swine					1			69		14	
Sheep											136

71

Table 22 (continued)

| | Regions | | | | | | | | | | |
Resources	1	2	3	4	5	6	7	8	9	10	11
Land (escudos per hectare)											
Olive	643		353	704	315	241	5,603	661	725	1,330	1,139
Grape	29,836	10,466	6,015	4,834	5,485	11,186		7,972			7,433
Oranges	9,125		5,272	6,830	3,883	4,052	1,346	593			
Pine	29			164				140		74	91
Eucalyptus	356			74							114
Cork		258			582		897	1,428	981	839	936
Irrigated						1,725	655	2,661		2,821	2,110
Other class A							139			440	
All class A			273		10			123	8		
Processing capacity (escudos per metric ton)[a]											
Beef	67,311		4,858					9,866			
Pork	99,472				96,294				77,739	70,816	
Lamb and mutton	196,394	61,431	77,980	61,368	149,148	55,883	78,346	82,504	160,002	157,485	90,944
Cow milk	2,560		2,116			2,500	2,641	2,648	1,076		
Sheep milk					15,790					15,784	
Cow milk for butter and cheese						537					

Meat storage (escudos per metric ton)[a]							
All meat	372,217	406,708	475,412	292,731	292,731	292,731	1,089,186
Fertilizer (escudos per kilogram)							
Nitrogen		0.42	0.80	0.74			
Phosphorous							
Forestry product processing (escudos per cubic meter)							
Lumber (pine)	350[b]						
Pulp (pine)	218	218		218		218	
Fiberboard (pine)	218	218	218		218		
Eucalyptus	227	227	227	227		227	

a. Capacity in critical months.
b. National constraint.

grammed unless the marginal cost is less than the shadow price, or marginal return.) Thus, for those regions which have positive shadow prices—3, 5, 6, 7—the cost per unit of machinery investment is greater than its shadow price.

Improvement of milk cow herds and of associated buildings and equipment also accounts for a large part of total prescribed investment —32 percent—in the variant 1 solution. Of this total, 95 percent is prescribed for regions 1 and 6, regions with a large concentration of population and therefore large demands for milk.

Some type of investment is designated for each region. Additional investments—for example, in beef, cattle, milk cows, hogs, sheep, and especially pine and eucalyptus forests—are prevented by the lack of some type of processing capacity. This result emphasizes the interdependency of investment decisions in a sectoral context. From a sectoral viewpoint many investment decisions must be considered in relation to other investments and their levels. Many times they must dovetail to be productive from a viewpoint of national welfare. Moreover, investments must be evaluated in relation to the expected demands for the products produced. In sectoral analysis, prices cannot be taken as constant or fixed. Thus, the amount of profitable investment is constrained by commodity demand.

In this vein it is now worthwhile to look more closely at the shadow prices of the fixed resources (see Table 22). The largest of these is for meat storage capacity, which in region 4 amounts to almost 500,000 escudos a metric ton. This figure may be a bit misleading because it relates to the maximum capacity at a specific time, in the most critical season. If the usual seasonal consumption patterns are maintained and capacity is expanded, higher consumption could occur throughout the year. Therefore, the shadow price is very high, because of which meat cold storage was not a constraint to the variant 2 analysis.

Meat processing facilities also have high shadow prices—for example, 196,000 escudos for lamb and mutton in region 7—and relate as well to critical months for slaughtering.

In the results obtained for 1968 surplus labor was the rule for all regions except 1, but in the 1980 results these surpluses disappear. In region 2 the supply of labor is exhausted in three out of the four quarters, while in regions 5 through 11 labor is constrained in two quarters. Despite the fact that labor is constraining, the marginal earnings, as indicated by the shadow prices, are low; the highest is about 18 escudos an hour during the fourth quarter in region 2. Farm wages of 18 escudos an hour are relatively high by 1960 standards, but they are not high in relation to projected 1980 regional income per capita.

Further irrigation development is not prescribed by the model results. Even though, for example, the shadow price (see Table 22) is quite high in region 10, it is much lower than the estimated total annual cost per hectare (irrigation development cost plus annual operating cost of delivering the water to the farmer). For region 10 this total cost amounted to 4,800 escudos as against a shadow price of 2,820 escudos. This shadow price per hectare must apply, of course, not only to the marginal irrigated unit but to all units produced by the irrigation development. In region 10 the irrigation development scheme encompassed 3,500 hectares. As the output from a large irrigation scheme expands, the prices of the products produced will fall. The amount of the price decline depends on the total quantity and package of products produced and their price elasticities of demand.

To this point no mention has been made of the integer or lumpy nature of investments or of the need for integer programming solutions. Except for irrigation, the integer values are so small with respect to the total level of investment that the changes resulting from exact integer solutions would be imperceptible. Because no irrigation development was specified in the continuous solution, it is an implicit integer solution.

The output of forestry products—lumber, fiberboard, and pulp—are limited or constrained for every region by processing capacity.[2] As a result, the shadow prices for wood processing facilities are quite high, in many cases nearly equal to the price to the producer (see Table 22). Thus, the opportunity costs are low, and it appears quite likely that investments in wood processing capacity would yield a high rate of return.

Only nitrogenous and phosphate fertilizers are produced in Portugal. Traditionally, the country has exported the former. Even if there were no additions by 1980, plant capacity for both nitrogen and phosphorous for domestic needs would be adequate according to the variant 1 solution. In the analysis no consideration was given to indigenous production to potash fertilizers. This may be something to be considered in further work.

Another image of the consequences of investments in agriculture is obtained by looking at the distribution of production among conventional and new techniques (see Table 23). The model prescriptions vary from commodity to commodity. Rice, oats, barley, string beans, and tomatoes are produced entirely by conventional techniques. On the other hand,

---

2. Each region does not have processing capacity for each of these products but can ship to other regions that have these facilities. In the solution, however, total country capacity is used up.

Table 23. Percentage of Commodities Programmed for Conventional and New Techniques of Production in the 1980 Model, Variant 1

Commodity	Conventional techniques	New techniques
Wheat	7	93
Rye	34	66
Maize	67	33
Rice	100	0
Oats	100	0
Barley	100	0
Chick-peas	26	74
Potatoes	79	21
String beans	100	0
Tomatoes	100	0
Beef	23	77
Pork	28	72
Mutton	29	71
Cow milk	39	71
Sheep milk	55	45
Wool	63	37
Forages	55	45

more than 90 percent of wheat is produced by new techniques. Some 84 percent of total wheat production would be from the southern part of the country, the Alentejo, where the terrain makes it possible to use large pieces of equipment and other advanced technology. Because they are part of the wheat rotation, chick-peas are produced mostly by advanced techniques in this same area. On the other hand, according to the model solution, two-thirds of rye and one-third of maize are to be produced by new techniques. These crops are produced largely in the northern part of the country. Given the complexity of the model, these results are not easy to explain, but the explanation probably lies in the labor supply. Traditional techniques use large amounts of labor and require small current cash expenditure and capital inputs. As long as labor is abundant, traditional methods will be more economical from the model's viewpoint—except in some cases in which total unit variable (cash) and capital costs of certain new techniques are less than those for traditional techniques. Thus, the new techniques replace the traditional techniques even with a zero shadow price for labor.

Table 24. Summary of Investment Activities in the 1980 Model, Variant 2

Resources	Regions 1	2	3	4	5	6	7	8	9	10	11	Total
Units supplied												
Farm mechanization (number of tractors)[a]	1,537.9			365.0		1,149.0	1,421.0		783.0	1,780.0	79.0	7,114.0
Milk cows (thousands)[b]	57.0			7.1		44.9			2.5	19.1	2.4	133.0
Beef cows (thousands)		39.3			13.9		41.5		44.9	8.6		148.2
Hogs (thousands)	8.0	1.4	3.9	0.7	5.8	4.5		0.4	6.1	40.3		71.1
Sheep (thousands)		17.0					257.3	155.9	224.2		130.5	784.9
Pine (thousands of hectares)				291.1								291.1
Eucalyptus (thousands of hectares)	84.4											84.4
Value (millions of escudos)												
Farm mechanization[c]	118.0			29.0		82.0	90.9		53.7	100.2	3.5	477.3
Milk cows	148.4			18.6		147.9			8.2	63.8	7.9	394.5
Beef cows		33.1			11.7		34.9		38.7	7.3		125.7
Hogs	10.4	1.8	5.1	0.9	7.6	5.8		0.5	8.0	52.5		92.6
Sheep		2.0					36.9	18.2	26.2		15.3	98.6
Pine				47.7								47.7
Eucalyptus	30.1											30.1
Total	306.9	36.9	5.1	96.2	19.3	235.7	162.7	18.7	134.8	223.8	26.7	1,266.8

a. In 50 horsepower tractor equivalent.
b. Units of female stock. Investment package includes other associate livestock, buildings, and equipment.
c. Includes cost of tractor and auxiliary equipment.

77

Table 25. Shadow Price of Resources in the 1980 Model, Variant 2

Resources	Region										
	1	2	3	4	5	6	7	8	9	10	11
Labor (escudos per hour)											
First quarter	2.65	1.41		6.38	3.65	9.16	26.17	1.11			1.61
Second quarter			2.16		1.85				12.60	0.96	2.69
Third quarter		2.66					5.84	4.36	6.17	7.41	
Fourth quarter		16.05									
Tractor (escudos per hour)											
First quarter	59.58				20.00						
Second quarter			54.39	5.65	20.37						
Third quarter						34.64	136.02				
Fourth quarter					13.63						
Animal power (escudos per hours)											
First quarter	2.71									1.87	
Second quarter			3.40	5.88				0.40			
Third quarter		3.74	6.81	2.95		4.97			5.03		
Fourth quarter					4.15			0.03			
Livestock inventory (escudos per head)											
Mules			1,524	1,185							
Bulls		862	2,560	2,182	1,135	951			1,206		1,437
Beef cows					135						885
Milk cows		142			704			90			1,422
Swine								1,259	453	38	
Sheep						39		54		1,765	134

Land (escudos per hectare)

Olive	602	339		689	270	44		508	400	1,221	1,091
Grape	29,894	5,705	11,514	4,842	6,140	11,263		7,894			7,071
Oranges	9,596	5,897		7,780	4,724	2,047	1,714	467		764	47
Pine	25			164				135			75
Eucalyptus	356			89		51			952	809	909
Cork			256		593		869	1,442		3,272	2,451
Irrigated						4,768	242	3,539		554	
Other class A					130			236	106		
All class A		243	13								

Processing capacity (escudos per metric ton)[a]

Beef	57,937	100,414			81,174			112,873	61,995	54,849	42,107
Pork	83,836	69,742						168,360	151,818	149,302	59,913
Lamb and mutton	189,477	157,348	140,091	140,452	141,073	141,739	164,310		952		171,256
Cow milk	2,542	2,077				2,439	2,513	2,631		15,818	
Sheep milk					15,963						

Fertilizer (escudos per kilogram)

Nitrogen	0.42			0.80							
Phosphorous						4.83		4.09			

Forestry product processing (escudos per cubic meter)

Lumber (pine)	350.00[b]										
Pulp (pine)	218.00	218.00		218.00	217.82	217.82	217.76	217.74			
Fiberboard (pine)	218.00	218.00		218.00			217.76	217.74			
Eucalyptus	225.41	225.23		225.08	225.08			225.05			

a. Capacity in critical months.
b. National constraint.

Variant 2

The release of constraints on storage capacity for meat permits a significant increase in production, especially of livestock products and particularly pork, which was imported under variant 1. As a result, significant additional investments are economic (see Table 24). Only two of the investment categories, sheep and eucalyptus, are prescribed at a lower level than for variant 1. The total level of investment would be increased by 22 percent. Investment in improved swine herds would be increased most, over 300 percent above that in variant 1. Larger cold-storage capacity for meat permits more of the pork consumed to be produced domestically rather than imported. In addition, domestic pork production is cheaper than imported pork when it is not constrained by the limits of cold-storage capacity.

Although many of the shadow prices change from variant 1 to variant 2, most of them increase (compare Tables 22 and 25). Those for processing meat and dairy products are relatively large compared with the cost of providing these types of facilities. (It must be noted again that the processing constraints are for critical months, and that the increase in maximum capacity has the effect of increasing through-put during all months.) Thus, the benefits are multiplied. In the model, two months out of the year during which production is greatest with respect to consumption are used as a processing constraint. Hence, the benefits of removing processing constraints are multiplied by a factor of six.

With additional investments, a larger percentage of the production of each crop is the result of new or advanced production techniques (see Table 26), as is expected. Investments are profitable because output by related production techniques is profitable, not vice versa. This is another way of saying that the demand for investment goods is a derived demand. The needed increases in cold-storage capacity required to implement the programmed output of variant 2 is 11,000 metric tons, or 40 percent above the base capacity of 1968 (which was 25,000 metric tons).

The net social payoff to this amount of investment in cold-storage facilities is 2.6 billion escudos in producer and consumer surplus, which compared with variant 1 represents an increase of about 8 percent in the net social payoff. Because most of the livestock products have price elasticities greater than 1, the net value of agricultural production (that is, total production valued at wholesale farm prices less production costs) increases by more than 5 percent. Finally, because the shadow price of cold-storage facilities is zero at the 36,000-metric ton level, the equilibrium amount used in variant 2, this amount of investment would not be

Table 26. Percentage of Commodities Programmed for Conventional and New Techniques of Production in the 1980 Model, Variant 2

Commodity	Conventional techniques	New techniques
Wheat	15	85
Rye	100	0
Maize	69	31
Rice	0	100
Oats	100	0
Barley	6	94
Chick-peas	0	100
Potatoes	66	34
String beans	100	0
Tomatoes	80	20
Beef	15	85
Pork	15	85
Mutton	27	73
Cow milk	25	75
Sheep milk	66	34
Wool	61	39
Forages	51	49

economical. In reality, one would want to stop short of this level, at a point at which the marginal social payoff would be just equal to the marginal cost.

Variant 3

A program is generated by variant 3 that also allows investment to proceed beyond the point at which marginal social payoff is just equal to marginal cost or to a point at which the shadow prices of slaughter, milk processing, and cold-storage capacities are zero. To reach this point, the following changes in processing capacity would need to take place relative to variant 2: for beef and veal, 9 percent; pork, 6 percent; lamb and mutton, 60 percent; cow milk, 65 percent; sheep milk, 54 percent; butter and cheese, 0.3 percent; and meat cold storage, 4 percent.

Thus, slaughter capacity for lamb and mutton and processing capacity for milk should be expanded most. Some additional investment in beef and pork processing also would probably be profitable. Moreover, when

Table 27. Summary of Investment Activities in the 1980 Model, Variant 3

Resources	Regions											Total
	1	2	3	4	5	6	7	8	9	10	11	
Units supplied												
Farm mechanization (number of tractors)[a]	1,537.0	309.0		912.0		1,394.0	1,487.0		783.0	1,767.0	63.0	8,252.0
Milk cows (thousands)[b]	57.1	5.1		17.8		57.9	1.6		2.1	18.7	2.4	162.0
Beef cows (thousands)		48.7					80.6		25.3			154.6
Hogs (thousands)	13.4	6.0	4.3		4.4	1.7		0.4	7.3	40.3		77.8
Sheep (thousands)		16.4			188.0		179.4	151.0	468.1	12.2	130.5	1,145.6
Pine (thousands of hectares)				277.0				1.2				278.2
Eucalyptus (thousands of hectares)	84.4											84.4
Value (millions of escudos)												
Farm mechanization[c]	118.0	17.1		72.7		99.9	95.7		53.7	99.7	2.5	559.3
Milk cows	148.4	13.4		46.3		191.0	5.5		6.9	62.5	7.9	481.9
Beef cows		41.0					67.8		21.8			130.6
Hogs	17.4	7.9	5.6		5.7	2.2		0.5	9.5	52.6		101.4
Sheep		1.9			22.0		21.0	17.7	54.8	1.4	15.3	134.1
Pine				45.4				0.2				45.6
Eucalyptus	30.1											30.1
Total	313.9	81.3	5.6	164.4	27.7	293.1	190.0	18.4	146.7	216.2	25.7	1,483.0

a. In 50 horsepower tractor equivalent.
b. Units of female stock. Investment package includes other associate livestock, buildings, and equipment.
c. Includes cost of tractor and auxiliary equipment.

processing capacity is expanded, the shadow price of investment in cold storage has again become positive, and would be expanded by about 4 percent above the variant 2 solution.

Increases in investments resulting from variant 3 compared with variant 2 follow the increased processing facilities allowed. Investments in milk cows and sheep herds increase by 22 and 46 percent, respectively (compare Tables 25 and 27). Additional livestock production requires more feed; hence, a higher level of investment in tractors and other machinery is profitable, amounting to 16 percent above that in variant 2.

Shadow prices of some fixed resources increase as the livestock production restraints are removed, as assumed in variant 3 (see Table 28). Irrigation development in region 6 has a high shadow price, 5,000 escudos a hectare. From a feasibility viewpoint, however, no further irrigation development was thought possible in this region. Hence, no irrigation investment activity was included in the model for region 6.

A summary of the methods of production derived for variant 3 is presented in Table 29.

Changes in the levels of investment result in changes in the levels of production. Although the production of most commodities increases as investments are increased from one variant to the other, some do not. When constraining resources that are product specific are allowed to increase, there may be a reduction in the output of some product using a common resource—say, labor—that constrains the total level of production.

Because of price changes among variants, it is difficult to give an overall measure of changes in the level of production, but an attempt was made to do this (see Table 30). (Note that the percentage increase in production from the 1968 base period changes markedly, depending on which price weights are used.) Only products common to all analyses are used to compute changes in total production.

Production in 1968 prices increases by 17 percent for variant 1, and since Portugal's total population is expected to decline slightly, per capita production would be higher in 1980 than in 1968 by a little more than 19 percent. On the other hand, if the prices generated by variant 1 are used to make the calculation, total production increases only 11 percent —the result of the fact that prices of a number of products decline because of large increases in production. Prices of products that remain the same or go up are those with the same or declining production—the results of a number of economic factors inherent in the model, including changing technology of production.

Table 28. Shadow Price of Resources in the 1980 Model, Variant 3

Resources						Regions					
	1	2	3	4	5	6	7	8	9	10	11
Labor (escudos per hour)											
First quarter	2.89	0.22		7.45	7.09	11.95	25.17	1.98	0.49		
Second quarter			2.78						13.87	3.46	2.62
Third quarter		3.65					5.15	3.30	5.60	8.11	1.99
Fourth quarter		16.03									
Tractor (escudos per hour)											
First quarter	94.19		62.74		13.35						
Second quarter		11.75		27.71	43.39						
Third quarter						62.56	155.66	1.31			2.45
Fourth quarter											
Animal power (escudos per hour)											
First quarter	2.72									2.62	
Second quarter		4.64	3.02	5.97				1.72			
Third quarter			4.43	2.47		5.34					
Fourth quarter					5.32			0.19	5.86		3.82
Livestock inventory (escudos per head)											
Mules			435	851							
Bulls		1,074	1,522	2,047	1,276	1,262		20	1,406		1,688
Beef cows											1,015
Milk cows					209		62	74			1,367
Swine								1,448	633	1,460	
Sheep	4				37	45		47			139

Land (escudos per hectare)

Olive	684	281	434	775	108			529	415	1,269	1,234
Grape	29,877	12,128	5,777	4,470	4,700	10,201		7,537			7,050
Oranges	9,830		6,040	8,015	4,658	1,855		399		542	
Pine	27			164			2,270	164			66
Eucalyptus	356			73		38					73
Cork		255			577			1,448	940	782	904
Irrigated						5,001	880	3,938		2,734	2,515
Other class A										715	
All class A		26	221		194		359	286	144		
Fertilizer (escudos per kilogram)											
Nitrogen			0.42	0.80	7.96						
Phosphorous								7.22			
Forestry product processing (escudos per cubic meter)											
Lumber (pine)	350.00[a]										
Pulp (pine)	218.00	218.00			217.82	217.76		217.74			
Fiberboard (pine)	218.00	218.00	218.00			217.76					
Eucalyptus	224.78	224.60			224.45			224.42			224.42

a. National constraint.

Table 29. Percentage of Commodities Programmed for Conventional and New Techniques of Production in the 1980 Model, Variant 3

Commodity	Conventional techniques	New techniques
Wheat	15	85
Rye	100	0
Maize	55	45
Rice	100	0
Oats	100	0
Barley	14	86
Chick-peas	26	74
Potatoes	47	53
String beans	100	0
Tomatoes	100	0
Beef	13	87
Pork	14	86
Mutton	24	76
Cow milk	21	79
Sheep milk	66	34
Wool	59	41
Forages	47	53

Table 30. Comparison of Total Value and Indexes of Production, Using Alternative Base Prices, for Model Solutions of 1968 and 1980, Selected Products [a]

Price base	1968, variant A-1	1980		
		Variant 1	Variant 2	Variant 3
1968				
Values (escudos)	26,992	31,683	36,928	38,829
Index	100	117	137	144
1980, variant 1				
Value (escudos)	22,635	25,177	—	—
Index	100	111	—	—
1980, variant 2				
Value (escudos)	22,984	—	28,938	—
Index	100	—	126	—
1980, variant 3				
Value (escudos)	21,760	—	—	27,526
Index	100	—	—	127

a. Wheat, rye, maize, rice, barley, chick-peas, potatoes, beans, oranges, olive oil, wine, beef, pork, mutton, milk, cheese, and butter.

Individual commodity details of production and prices are presented in Tables 31 and 32, which show that production of wheat and animal products have the greatest increase. The production of feed grains, maize and barley, in the 1980 model are programmed below the 1968 level because a large percentage of livestock products are produced by more efficient stocks of animals that are provided by the investment activities. This means that the gain, or production per unit of feed, is higher than that for traditional herds. Pork production in the 1980 model under

Table 31. Total Commodity Production in the 1968 Model (Variant A-1) and the 1980 Model (All Variants)
(Thousands of metric tons or liters)

| Commodity | 1968, variant A-1 | 1980 | | |
		Variant 1	*Variant 2*	*Variant 3*
Wheat	262.3	792.7	787.6	788.4
Rye	164.3	94.9	102.9	98.3
Maize	669.9	421.4	558.6	665.7
Rice	229.0	215.4	172.5	110.0
Barley	109.8	54.4	98.5	77.3
Chick-peas	8.9	10.8	10.7	10.7
Potatoes	906.3	618.0	618.0	618.0
Beans	52.7	20.8	24.6	21.0
Oranges	106.9	164.3	164.3	164.3
Olive oil	59.2	55.4	55.4	54.2
Wine	1,162.9	1,134.4	1,123.6	1,113.5
Tomatoes	750.0	1,087.0	887.3	885.7
Melons	—ᵃ	30.0	30.0	30.0
Beef	50.5	139.8	159.3	174.9
Pork	104.4	46.3	174.3	188.3
Mutton	25.1	35.9	35.9	54.1
Milk	354.9	658.4	640.5	742.0
Cheese	21.2	31.3	31.3	30.3
Butter	1.9	2.5	2.5	2.9
Wool	11.3	6.4	7.0	8.9
Vegetable oil	—ᵃ	120.0	120.0	120.0
Cork	—ᵃ	35.9	35.9	35.9
Resin	—ᵃ	100.0	100.0	99.3
Pine logs ᵇ	—ᵃ	10.2	10.2	10.2
Eucalyptus ᵇ	—ᵃ	2.2	2.2	2.2

a. Not included in the 1968 model.
b. In millions of cubic meters.

**Table 32. Average Prices of Commodities, 1968 and 1980,
for Three Variants**
(Escudos)

Commodity	1968, variant A-1	1980 Variant 1	Variant 2	Variant 3
Wheat	7.06	3.06	3.19	3.13
Rye	6.03	3.74	3.30	3.49
Maize	3.99	1.96	3.97	3.97
Rice	5.43	4.98	5.14	5.25
Barley	5.19	4.26	4.77	4.93
Chick-peas	10.12	5.09	5.09	5.09
Potatoes	1.47	1.40	1.40	1.40
Beans	10.87	13.61	13.60	13.60
Oranges	7.41	3.31	3.31	3.31
Olive oil	22.10	17.92	17.92	19.16
Wine	5.83	5.89	5.87	5.89
Beef	32.60	31.28	23.02	17.08
Pork	30.89	30.59	24.73	22.39
Mutton	40.54	46.60	46.60	30.94
Milk	4.26	3.81	3.81	2.45
Cheese	61.43	31.21	31.22	37.17
Butter	44.70	23.23	23.21	23.17

variant 1 is less than for 1968 because the cold-storage capacity is used for beef instead of pork, which means that beef has a higher net social payoff than pork.

According to the model solutions, interregional trade would, in a relative sense, be at a higher level in 1980 than in 1968 (see Table 33). The commodities affected most are wheat and animal products, in part because of a reduction in imports, which substitute for interregional trade, in part because of regional specialization that results from new production techniques. On the other hand, interregional trade decreases for some products, such as rice—the result of higher imports than in the base year, 1968.

Changes in interregional trade patterns, though somewhat academic, are important for planning transport. We have assumed that transport facilities would not be constraining because agriculture is a small part of the total economy. If the model encompassed the entire economy, it would be relatively easy to include transport constraints in the analysis.

Table 33. Average per Capita Consumption of Commodities, 1968 and 1980, for Three Variants
(Kilograms or liters)

Commodity	1968, variant A-1	1980		
		Variant 1	*Variant 2*	*Variant 3*
Wheat [a]	63.6	79.3	78.8	78.9
Rye [a]	11.4	9.0	9.8	9.4
Maize [a]	27.9	27.8	24.6	24.6
Rice [a]	17.0	20.0	19.8	19.6
Barley [a]	0.2	0.3	0.2	0.2
Chick-peas	1.2	1.3	1.3	1.3
Potatoes	105.7	77.3	77.3	77.3
Beans	5.3	2.6	3.1	2.6
Oranges	12.5	20.6	20.6	20.6
Olive oil [a]	3.9	3.8	3.8	3.7
Wine [a]	91.9	79.4	78.5	78.5
Beef [b]	8.3	17.6	20.3	21.9
Pork [b]	12.6	20.6	22.7	23.5
Mutton [b]	2.7	4.3	4.3	6.6
Milk	22.6	42.9	42.9	60.6
Cheese [a]	2.5	3.9	3.9	3.8
Butter [a]	0.6	0.3	0.3	0.4

a. Processed weight.
b. Carcass weight.

FOREIGN TRADE

The pattern of imports changes markedly in the 1980 model results in comparison with that of 1968 (compare Tables 13 and 35). There are no longer any wheat and maize imports and only a small amount of beef. But imports of rice are now specified, and pork imports are increased dramatically—the latter as mentioned above, because there is a shortage of cold-storage capacity. The patterns of exports do not change for 1980 in variant 1. The level exports are higher because the constraints were set higher than for 1968 in the expectation that export demand for the products would grow. For all three variants the agricultural trade balance is positive, increasing from 1.8 billion escudos for variant 1 to 4.2 for variant 2—the result of a sharp drop in imports as exports drop but slightly under variant 2. With no constraint in cold-storage capacity,

Table 34. Percentage of Domestic Production Traded Interregionally, 1968 and 1980 Models

Commodity	1968, variant A-1	1980		
		Variant 1	Variant 2	Variant 3
Wheat	37	71	76	75
Rye	49	40	60	62
Maize	25	49	34	38
Rice	74	56	45	21
Oats	0	12	7	8
Barley	24	27	56	21
Chick-peas	70	86	86	86
Potatoes	47	37	12	25
Beans	30	79	65	73
Oranges	69	41	41	44
Olive oil	28	29	24	31
Wine	16	13	14	14
Beef	24	47	55	52
Pork	33	86	72	64
Mutton	63	79	69	69
Milk	18	13	15	14
Cheese	30	36	47	29
Butter	5	0	0	24

livestock production for domestic consumption competes with tomato exports; consequently, tomato exports are lower under variant 2.

The total value of imports specified by variant 3 is slightly higher than for variant 2 (see Tables 36 and 37). Imports of rice, high-protein feed, and potash are also all higher. Exports, on the other hand, are lower: specifically, tomato products and wine. As a whole, the balance of trade is about 2 percent lower for the products considered. These data serve to point out that changes in critical resources could have a large impact on optimal trade patterns from a country point of view.

LIMITATIONS

The foregoing result highlights a number of limitations in analysis.

First, in some regions a few commodities are not produced at market equilibrium levels, because the range of prices chosen to represent the

Table 35. Agricultural Balance of Payments in the 1980 Model, Variant 1

Commodity	Quantity (metric tons or thousands of liters)	Value (thousands of escudos)
Imports		
Rice	9,288	31,208
Beef	691	20,730
Pork	117,999	2,949,975
Potash	50,390	151,170
Total		3,153,083
Exports		
Tomato products	200,000 [a]	1,400,000
Olive oil	25,000 [a]	537,500
Wine	500,000 [a]	3,000,000
Lamb	1,500 [a]	78,750
Total		5,016,250
Trade balance		1,863,167

a. Constrained at export limit.

Table 36. Agricultural Balance of Payments in the 1980 Model, Variant 2

Commodity	Quantity (metric tons or thousands of liters)	Value (thousands of escudos)
Imports		
Rice	37,230	125,093
Beef	691	20,730
Pork	6,747	168,675
High-protein feed	30,341	98,608
Potash	51,786	155,358
Total		568,464
Exports		
Tomato products	163,262	1,142,834
Olive oil	25,000 [a]	537,500
Wine	495,815	2,974,890
Lamb	1,500 [a]	78,750
Total		4,733,974
Trade balance		4,161,510

a. Constrained at export limit.

Table 37. Agricultural Balance of Payments in the 1980 Model, Variant 3

Commodity	Quantity (metric tons or thousands of liters)	Value (thousands of escudos)
Imports		
Rice	79,842	268,269
High-protein feed	46,370	150,703
Potash	53,784	161,352
Total		580,324
Exports		
Tomato products	162,970	1,140,790
Olive oil	25,000 [a]	537,500
Wine	485,717	2,914,302
Lamb	1,500 [a]	78,750
Total		4,671,342
Trade balance		4,091,018

a. Constrained at export limit.

demand function was in the wrong segment of the demand function. In some cases, production may have been specified for a particular product in a particular region if the maximum price had been increased in the objective function; in other cases, a lower price may have been specified if the maximum amount sold, as specified by the constraint row, had been increased.

Second, the results probably would be improved if labor supply functions were used in the place of fixed availability of labor. It is doubtful whether, given the shadow prices derived, labor would be available at the level of employment specified in each region.

Third, for all replaceable resources there should have been investment activities. It is difficult and time consuming to obtain investment or construction cost data for such items as slaughterhouses, milk processing plants, and cold-storage facilities. Estimates for such costs often require an engineering study.

Fourth, because the model is static, it is not possible to give a realistic characterization of the investment program in any time dimension. The size of dynamic programming matrixes increases geometrically as the number of years used in the analysis increases. Costs, therefore, increase rapidly, and computer capacity is quickly reached.

Conceptually, we can deal with each of these defects; only time, resources, and computer capability prevent us from doing so. The first and second limitations can be corrected easily and economically; the third and fourth are more difficult to handle appropriately.

COMPARISON OF MODEL AND MISSION RECOMMENDATIONS

One of the important objectives of this study was to compare the results of the models with the recommendations of the agricultural sector mission to Portugal in 1969. The mission made many wide-ranging and broad recommendations for administration and policy: for example, for a reorganization in the Agricultural Department and lower price supports for wheat. But such items are outside the scope of this analysis, which deals only with the technical and economic aspects of agricultural programs. The mission also made certain recommendations that are related to the prescriptions of this study. These may be summarized as follows:

—A program to plant a total 140,000 hectares in eucalyptus trees over a period of ten years

—Programs of beef cattle and sheep production that would include establishment of subterranean clover pastures, improvement of basic breeding herds, and expansion of livestock slaughter facilities

—Investments in cold-storage plants for fruits and meat

—Investments in port facilities

The mission made no recommendation for investments in irrigation schemes. It did, however, recommend that a task force be employed to evaluate thoroughly the current irrigation development plan. The mission was skeptical of a number of individual projects.

Except for development of eucalyptus forests, each of these recommendations was only qualitative, a factor that is one of the significant differences between the mission's recommendation and the model's specifications. Qualitatively, the second and third recommendations above, are consistent with the analysis presented in this report. But there is missing not only the quantitative aspect but also the locational specification, which is of great importance in any development program. The mission report made no recommendation for development of pine forests or forestry processing facilities, two items that appear to have a favorable rate of return. Moreover, as a result of our analysis, we would recommend the development of swine production as well as cattle and sheep. The possibility for investments in tractor and other labor-saving machinery was not explicitly considered in the mission report. According to the model results, this type of investment is economic in six of the eleven regions. In addition, there was no mention of expansion of dairy cattle herds, which is specified for four of the eleven regions in the model's results. It is not surprising that most of this investment is prescribed for regions 1 and 6, in which 50 percent of total population is expected to live in 1980.

Another matter that was ignored in the mission report was new crop development—except for subterranean clover. According to our analysis, Portugal could compete with overseas producers of vegetable oil seeds, which supply high-protein meal feeds and food oils. These, according to the model results, could be supplied through sunflower and safflower production. Domestic production of these crops could replace a large volume of the historical imports of oil meals and vegetable oils.

In summary, the mission's recommendations are qualitatively consistent with our analysis for the investment for certain development categories, but there are a number of omissions in its recommendations. These include dairy, swine, pine forest, wood product processing, and agricultural machinery. Furthermore, except in one case, the mission prescriptions lack the quantification and locational dimensions, which are essential elements of practical development programs.

Bibliography

Ablasser, Gottfried, and Alvin C. Egbert. *Brazil Agricultural Sector Planning Model: An Application of Mathematical Regional Programming: A Summary Report.* Agriculture and Rural Development Department Working Paper no. 1. Washington, D.C.: World Bank, December 1973.

Alves, Antonio Monteiro da Silva, and Fernando Gomes. *A Contribuicão do Sector Agricola Para O Desenvolvimento Economico em Portugal,* série A. 18. Lisbon: Fundação Calouste Gulbenkian, Centro de Estudos de Economia Agrária, Lisboa Publicaçoes, 1965.

Banco Portugues do Atlantico. *Alguns Aspectos da Economia Portuguesa.* Lisbon: Banco Portugues do Atlantico, 1966.

Brokken, Ray F., and Earl O. Heady. *Interregional Adjustments in Crops and Livestock Production.* U.S. Department of Agriculture Technical Bulletin no. 1396. Washington, D.C.: Government Printing Office, 1968.

Campilhas, Perimetro de. *Estudo Economico-Social das Obras de Fomento Hidragoagricola.* Lisbon: Secretaria de Estado da Agricultura, 1961.

Carvalho, Cardoso, and U. J. Jose. *Os Solos de Portugal: Sua Classificacão e Genese. 1. A Sul do Rio Tejo.* Lisbon: Secretaria de Estado da Agricultura, 1965.

Cary, Francisco Caldena. *Tempos: Padroes de Trabalho Para a Cultura Arvense de Sequeiro no Alentejo.* Lisbon: Fundação Calouste Gulbenkian, Centro de Estudos de Economia Agrária, 1965.

Castro Caldas, Eugenio de, and Manuel de Santos Loureiro. *Niveis de Desenvolvimento Agricola.* Lisbon: Fundação Calouste Gulbenkian, *No Continente Portugues,* 1963.

95

Dorfman, Robert, Paul A. Samuelson, and Robert Solow. *Linear Programming and Economic Analysis*. New York: McGraw-Hill Book Co., 1958.

Egbert, A. C., and Earl O. Heady. *Regional Analysis of Production Adjustments in Major Field Crops: Historical and Prospective*. U.S. Department of Agriculture Technical Bulletin no. 1294. Washington, D.C.: Government Printing Office, 1963.

Fox, Karl. "A Spatial Equilibrium Model of the Livestock Feed Economy in the United States." *Econometrica*, 21:547–66, 1953.

Goreaux, Louis M. *Multi-Level Programming in the Ivory Coast*. World Bank report in process.

Goreaux, Louis M., and Alan S. Manne, eds. *Multi-Level Planning: Case Studies in Mexico*. Amsterdam: North-Holland Publishing Co., 1973.

Heady, Earl O., ed. *Economic Models and Quantitative Methods for Decision and Planning in Agriculture*. Proceedings of an East-West Seminar, held in Keszthely, Hungary, Summer 1969. Ames, Iowa: Iowa State University Press, 1971.

Instituto Nacional de Estatistica. *Estatisticas Agricolas*. Lisbon: Instituto Nacional de Estatistica, 1953–1970.

Lopaz, Cardoso A. *Le Portugal, Structures Agraires et Systeme Politique, Analyse Prevision*. Paris: n.d.

Losch, August. *The Economics of Location*. New Haven: Yale University Press, 1954.

Lourenco, J. Silva, and Vitor Manuel Alves. *Tempos de Trabalho Agricola Numa Regiao de Noroeste*. Lisbon: Fundação Calouste Gulbenkian, Centro de Estudos de Economia Agrária, 1968.

Ministerio das Financas. *The Portuguese Tax System*. Lisbon: Centro de Estudos Fiscais, 1966.

Organization for Economic Cooperation and Development. *Food Consumption Statistics 1960–1968*. Paris: OECD, 1970.

————. *Production of Fruits and Vegetables in OECD Member Countries: Present Situation and Prospects, Portugal*. Paris: OECD, 1967.

————, Documentation in Agriculture and Food. *Co-operative Research on Input/Output Relationships in Beef Production*. Paris: OECD, 1968.

Pintado, V. X. *Structure & Growth of the Portuguese Economy*. Geneva: European Free Trade Association, 1964.

Planungsgruppe Ritter. *Portugal, Reseau National des Abattoirs*, vols. 1–6. Konigstun: Allemage, October 1968.

Samuelson, Paul A. "Spatial Price Equilibrium and Linear Programming." *American Economic Review,* 42:283–303, 1952.

Schrader, L. F., and G. A. King. "Regional Location of Beef Cattle Feeding." *Journal of Farm Economics,* 44:64–81, 1962.

Takayama, T., and G. G. Judge. "Spatial Equilibrium and Quadratic Programming." *Journal of Farm Economics,* 46:67–93, 1966.

Theil, H. *Economic Forecasts and Policy.* Amsterdam: North-Holland Publishing Co., 1961.

World Bank. *Agricultural Sector Survey: Portugal.* 2 vols., restricted circulation. Washington, D.C.: International Bank for Reconstruction and Development, 1970.

Yaron, Dan, Yakir Plessner, and Earl O. Heady. "Competitive Equilibrium: Application of Mathematical Programming." *Canadian Journal of Agricultural Economics,* vol. 13, no. 2, 1965.